Managing From the Heart

by

Hyler Bracey

Jack Rosenblum

Aubrey Sanford

Roy Trueblood

HEART Enterprises

Atlanta, Georgia

Printed in the United States of America

Book Design by Mary LaBoy

Acknowledgements

We gratefully acknowledge:

Our wives, Cass Flagg, Corinne Dugas, Kay Sanford, and Jackie Trueblood for lovingly supporting us through thick and thin in bringing the message of managing from the heart to the world.

The staff and senior consultants of The Atlanta Consulting Group for their dedication and creativity in helping managers learn how to manage from the heart.

Our clients, for having provided us with opportunities to test our ideas, for giving us feedback on what has worked and what has not worked for them, and for encouraging us to write this book and make the concept of managing from the heart available to a wider public.

Louis Savary, whose inspired editorial assistance helped create the miracle of turning the four of us into novelists.

Each other, for persevering in a relationship that, in its ups and downs and in its steadfast commitment to each other, constitutes an amazingly successful four-way professional marriage.

Hyler Bracey
Jack Rosenblum
Aubrey Sanford
Roy Trueblood

Introduction

*M*anaging *From the Heart* is a book for managers, and it is about *heart,* the universal symbol of caring and compassion.

In general, what managers do is plan for, train, and motivate employees within the perspective of their company's mission or vision of the future. What makes managers *effective* is doing their job with competence, confidence, and caring.

Everyone agrees that competence and confidence in a manager make a lot of sense.

"But caring?" someone asks. "How does that fit in?"

We believe that a company cannot maintain high-quality people, products, and profits unless it is managed with compassion and caring. While these qualities are crucial in effective management, their role is often misunderstood. If you did a survey of managers, most would say that they *do* care. The difficulty arises in the expression of that caring. It's not that managers need to care more, but that they need to learn to make their care more evident and express it more effectively.

Though most managers, from firsthand experience, can describe the differences in effectiveness between caring and uncaring bosses, many have difficulty themselves managing with care and compassion. This state of affairs has probably been spawned by some common misconceptions.

One misconception says that since caring is only an attitude it is of little importance. To some managers, caring compassionately about people is a quality that ranks lowest on their list. Some would even assert it has no place in business, and they have no time to waste learning about it. On the other hand, we say that a manager's effectiveness on the job is severely handicapped without compassion and caring.

Another misconception is that caring is soft and, therefore, ineffective behavior. On the contrary, caring may call for some of the "toughest" behavior employees can experience. When you truly care, you give both positive and negative feedback, you demand excellent performance rather than tolerate a poor job, you allow employees to profit from their mistakes and learn from new situations, and you encourage independence rather than dependence.

A third misconception is that caring behavior is easy to express, even for someone who's never attempted it before. However, caring behaviors are learned behaviors. For most of us, they don't come naturally. Like any skill, showing care takes practice. With practice, a manager can learn to function with such skill that employees consistently maintain and even enhance their self-worth and productivity.

A fourth misconception is that caring and compassion don't belong in the marketplace. We believe there are many ways to show caring appropriately—through a genuine concern for others, a sensitivity to their feelings and wishes, enthusiasm at their successes, excitement at their achievements at home as well as at work, support in time of need, camaraderie in time of accomplishment, a commitment to being honest with them, time and effort freely given to help them succeed at their tasks, to mention a few examples.

There is more purpose to our lives than just making money, wielding power or always coming out on top. This book is based on a belief that we are all on the journey together, and the best way to survive, prosper, and enjoy the trip is to do it together, and to do it from the heart, loving and respecting each other.

That goes for managers, too. For many managers today, the interpersonal quality of their relationships with other managers, employees, customers, suppliers, and even competitors has reached a crucial turning point.

People on the job are not meant to be criticized, bullied, threatened, constantly evaluated, and inspected. Workers do not want to spend their daily nine-to-five in an unhealthy stressful atmosphere, living under constant pressure or getting burned out in the prime of life. The human spirit was not designed to be the recipient of such disrespect and abuse. Yet in a very real way we watch things like this happen _unnecessarily_ every day in offices, meeting rooms, factories, and assembly lines. One big reason they happen by default is that managers have not learned to manage from the heart.

Deep down, what we all really want to see at work are fellow employees eagerly spending their energies, working alone and together, to create meaningful products and services that will make a difference in the lives of people. As humans, we are meant to work, to expend effort, to create. We are also meant to find satisfaction in doing our jobs competently, to value and be valued, to challenge each other to live to our highest potential, to make sure everyone succeeds, to prosper together peacefully. This can happen best in a caring, compassionate work environment. But it won't happen until a majority of managers begin to manage effectively from the heart, until it is the commonly accepted practice of business to operate in this manner.

Our goal in this book is to show managers a simple and direct way to open their hearts. Managing from the heart is the way we see caring and respect being spread throughout the business world.

Hyler Bracey
Jack Rosenblum
Aubrey Sanford
Roy Trueblood

Contents

Harry's Experience

As Harry Hartwell strode through his Ramoco oil refinery on his daily tour of inspection, he greeted everyone by name, yet never slowed his pace.

"Hi, Harry. How's it going?" said one of the supervisors, an old-timer in the oil business like Harry.

"I'm going great, George," his voice boomed in reply, as he kept moving forward. "But the big question is how's it going with that wounded Number 4 tower?" He smiled at George and pointed at the distillation tower that hadn't been running to capacity for almost a month.

George got the message.

As they saw Harry's large frame approaching, workers made sure they were working, visibly doing something productive. Sometimes conversations stopped until he was well past. He didn't make comments out loud to everyone, as he did to George. Usually his look would say it all.

"Good morning, Mr. Hartwell," said a young woman, turning from a bank of instruments to face the refinery manager, her eyeglasses slowly slipping down her nose. The younger employees did not feel free to call him by his first name.

"It'll be a _great_ morning, Teri, if you can tell me that you've finally mastered those reactor adjustments."

Harry had passed by before Teri could give her embarrassed reply.

A trio of maintenance people on their hands and knees around an ailing machine heard Harry's voice coming around the bend. "Let's get moving," said the one wearing a baseball cap. "Here comes the Field Marshall." He stirred noisily in his tool box to find the proper sized wrench.

His companion replied in a half-kidding voice, "When Harry comes by, it's the fastest you move all day."

The third maintenance man whispered to the first, since Harry was approaching, "Look who's talking." He pointed a screwdriver at the second man and said to him, "If Harry did inspections twice a day, you'd be twice as productive." Then he looked up to smile at Harry and in a louder voice asked, "Hey, Harry. Whatsa' matter with the Giants?"

"Probably the same thing that's wrong with your maintenance team, Joe. Too slow on the uptake."

Almost three decades ago, the university had trained Harry to be a chemical engineer and a varsity fullback. His diploma got him a job as a process engineer at Ramoco, the oil refinery his father was managing. His gridiron experience helped to advance his career. A 250-pound fullback's strategy is quite simple: Put your head down and run through the hole in the line; keep driving toward the goal until somebody stronger than you stops you; and never let go of the ball. During the past quarter-century, using this basic strategy he had been making steady gains until, like his father, he now sat at the head of the same hometown Ramoco Oil Refinery.

He loved the oil business. At ten years old, he knew by name every piece of equipment in his father's refinery. At the Ramoco Anniversary Party last Saturday night, he had regaled a group of employees with stories from the old days at Ramoco, stories that made them laugh at the crazy things that had happened in their refinery and some of the characters who had worked there. At such moments, folks could feel proud to be part of Harry's team. But these moments were rare on the job, where he was more often seen as intimidating.

As Harry's deep voice echoed ahead of him, two junior managers, a man and a woman, were carrying on a conversation in front of the vending machines at the far end of the long corridor.

"Have you proposed your new idea to Harry yet?" the woman asked the man, realizing it would be half a minute before Harry reached the place where they were standing.

"I've decided to wait a bit," the young man replied. "I don't think the Abominable No Man would go for another capital expenditure this quarter."

"I thought you said he was a straight shooter. Why hesitate?"

"He is a straight shooter, but he pulls the trigger a whole lot. And I don't want to be a sitting target. From Harry, a No is not just a No, it earns you a place on his Dumb Ideas List."

"Quiet," she whispered as she put her finger to her lips. "Here comes the old man now."

Both junior managers stood up straight, smiled, and exchanged polite greetings with Harry as he passed by. His thick eyebrows, square jaw, and wide mouth gave him the air of someone rugged, ruddy, and strong. People at the refinery, however, often saw those features as the marks of a gruff, formidable boss.

As soon as Harry had passed out of earshot, the young man continued, "I'd like to find a way out of this place. When that guy looks at you, you feel he is either going to take your name or kick your butt."

Harry entered his spacious office and sat down at his desk. At first, his mind drifted to the promotion he was bucking for—Vice President of U.S. Operations was his next objective. But the pressure there was stronger than ever. That got him to thinking about the problems he faced at the refinery and some obstacles facing him in his own life. He felt vaguely troubled. Recently, his body had been giving him subtle messages of stress: shortness of breath, frequent colds, and a lingering cough. At breakfast that morning, his wife Molly had expressed concern that he seemed depressed about something.

Lately, too, he had been tormented by a recurring nightmare about losing control. In the dream he would be driving his car to work. As he approached a red light and tried to stop, he would press the brake pedal but, instead of stopping, the car would rev its engine and accelerate. To avoid hitting other cars going through the intersection he would then quickly turn the steering wheel, but it would spin uselessly in his hands. Amid screeching brakes and honking horns, his car would swerve unpredictably and careen toward other cars. A split-second before the crash, he would wake in a cold sweat. At other times when he had the dream, his car would smash through the guard rail of a bridge and he would be plunging toward imminent death. When he awoke from these nightmares shuddering, he wondered who or what disruptive force was trying to destroy his life.

He didn't have to look very far. For Harry, waking life held a lot of threatening problems, people he didn't want to see and and situations he didn't want to deal with. During the past week alone, disgruntled machinists' union representatives had come waving an almost-expired labor contract in his face, a fax had notified him that the next ten million barrels of crude for his refinery would be delayed while a tanker was being repaired, the state environmental agency's letter on his desk hinted at evidence that his refinery was polluting the local air, and upper management at Ramoco headquarters had called for an immediate across-the-board 15 percent cut in the salaried staff. But these problems were his usual diet. Dealing with the unexpected was what a general manager at a refinery did.

Unlike some of his more conniving colleagues who had risen in the Ramoco hierarchy, Harry did not play office politics. At board meetings, higher management spoke admiringly of his no-nonsense style and workaholism. His refinery was almost always tops in production and was always tops in turnover, giving it a middling position in profitability.

As Harry leaned back in his chair pondering his responsibilities to the refinery, he pictured himself conducting his next inspection tour dressed in Western attire and riding around on a horse, with a silver badge on his shirt that said, "Ramoco Sheriff." He sighed. To him, the law-enforcer image was not funny, it was wearying. "I guess my job here is to dispense frontier justice." It was the voice of a man who knew what he had to do and didn't want to do it. But the bottom line was that he loved the oil business. "I want the refinery to succeed because it is my life."

The refinery was indeed his life. In fact, the standing joke was that Harry had an oil pump for a heart and oil in his veins. Once when he cut himself, there was a spirited debate about the octane level of the emerging fluid.

But that hypothesis didn't hold up. Oil does not form clots in key arteries.

At a meeting later that day while he was announcing a schedule of layoffs, Harry keeled over and was rushed to the hospital. He remained in a coma on life-support systems.

H‌arry awoke seated in a chair in a waiting room decorated in varying shades of white. White floor, white walls, white furniture—the entire room was bathed in a shimmering white light. He recognized it was not a hospital room, because the place had a strange, unearthly air about it. He shook his head as if trying to clear his mind and his vision.

He looked down. His hairy arms and legs stuck out of a covering of white material, which he did not at first recognize as a hospital gown. "Oh shit, I've bought the farm," he thought. "I've kicked the bucket. Just when the refinery was ready to shoot ahead."

"It can't be!" he said, trying to argue himself out of his first thoughts. "I'm healthy as a horse! I gotta' get outa' here!"

As his vision cleared, he noticed there was a person seated in a chair directly across from him. It was a woman of indeterminate age with warm, sparkling eyes.

Harry jumped up from his chair and moved toward her.

"Where am I?" he asked. "What is this weird place? I don't know if I'm dead or dreaming. Can you get me out of here? I've got a new shift coming on with a reduced work force. I gotta' get back right now!"

She remained calmly seated. "Sit down, Harry," she said. "You're not going anywhere right now." She raised her arm gracefully and pointed to his seat.

He felt her authority and followed her instruction.

"That's better," she said smiling. "If you'll listen, I'll explain your situation." She smoothed the white robe at her knee. "You fall into what we call our 'discretionary category.'"

"What the hell is that?" he demanded, with his head bulled forward. Charm had never been Harry's long suit.

"You seem upset," she replied gently. "I'll explain."

Harry moved to the edge of his seat, his big hands squeezing the arms of his chair. He had to keep his wits about him. He still didn't know where she was coming from and how he could get out of there.

"Imagine for a moment," she continued, "without objecting or arguing, that the purpose of life is spiritual growth and learning, particularly learning about loving. In those terms, Harry Hartwell, your life has reached a dead end. You are doing the same things over and over. At work you are intimidating and frustrating each new group of managers. Your family life has a rigid, set pattern. Nothing is changing. You might as well be dead."

"That's not true! We had to change lots of things at Ramoco. For example, the oil shortage in the 70's, the glut of the 80's, going into high gear on no-lead gasoline production, force reduction. Lots of things change all the time and we have to change with them." Harry felt he had made a telling point.

"Circumstances have changed, Harry, but you haven't. There is no point in my returning you to continue more of the same. It would be a waste of my discretionary power."

"Is she saying the ball game is over?" he growled to himself, shifting his eyes like a cornered animal, desperate to find a way out of this mess.

"So where's the 'discretionary' part?" he asked finally, looking at her. Harry had done a lot of labor negotiations for management, so he decided his strategy would be to negotiate for a new lease on life. He forced his lips into the shape of a smile. "What would I have to do to get back again?"

"Good, Harry." She smiled genuinely. "That's the right question. The truth is we are not neutral observers here. We have a mission that involves re-creating the world with more love and compassion in it, establishing a norm of love in all human transactions. Because of this mission, we are given discretion in certain cases. We can send a few people back whom we believe can help spread some love in the world."

Harry jumped from his seat, and his hospital gown billowed. "Why should love be the only criterion?" he asked, moving toward her. "And how could you measure it? It's too soft, too mushy, too wimpy even. How about production? America and, really, the whole world depends on oil. What if I can go back and increase our production by 25 percent?"

Harry had no idea how he could increase production at that rate in an old-design refinery, but he was willing to try. He was willing to promise anything just to get back to his familiar world.

"I'm sorry, but even if you could double fuel production, it wouldn't matter to us. The discretionary category relates only to the production of love in the world, and to date your production has been minimal."

"I don't even know what you're talking about," Harry muttered, turning away.

"I know you don't. Let's talk about your role as a manager which has occupied most of your waking hours and attention. Up until now you have managed with logic and anger from your head and your spleen. You have used statistical analyses, market forecasts, economic indicators—all head tools. And you have used and abused superior position power, bullying, ridicule, and put-downs—all spleen tools. What you have *not* done is manage from the heart."

"Manage from the heart?" He was shouting now. "That's a contradiction in terms right there. How can you manage from your heart? Even if you could, the workers and the competition, not to mention the oil-producing countries, would eat you alive."

"I know that's what you believe, Harry, or at least what you fear would happen. But managing from the heart is the way we see love being spread in the world through business."

"Okay," he said, turning with a smile to face her. She had just offered him a new line of argument. "Suppose somebody wanted to manage from the heart. How would they put it into practice? Just tell me how they'd do it, in good operational language." He grinned and sat down again, then looked at her. "I'm waiting."

"Managing from the heart may be expressed as five principles," she began without hesitation. "Think of them as five requests everyone at work makes of you:

1. Please don't make me wrong, even if you disagree.

2. Hear and understand me.

3. Tell me the truth with compassion.

4. Remember to look for my loving intention.

5. Acknowledge the greatness within me."

1. *Please don't make me wrong, even if you disagree.*

2. *Hear and Understand me.*

3. *Tell me the truth with compassion.*

4. *Remember to look for my loving intention.*

5. *Acknowledge the greatness within me.*

He was surprised that she had an actual plan, even if he saw it as hopelessly utopian. He shook his head, rejecting her principles. "Like I said, they would eat you alive," he concluded, grinning smugly. He knew firsthand the pervasive win/lose mentality of the business world. "This heart business doesn't fly with today's workers, with unions and all. You've got to be hard-headed. You give them an inch and they'll take a mile. You show weakness and they're all over you like white on rice."

"We have a growing number of managers out there living their lives according to these principles," she replied, "and far from getting eaten alive, they're actually doing quite well. You could be one of them." She smiled at Harry.

Harry squirmed and fidgeted through all of this, rubbing his chin, scratching his head.

"Look," he finally said, "believe it or not I have a heart. Ask my wife Molly if you don't believe me. She knows. We've been together 27 years."

"Harry, I know very well you have a heart. That's why I'm hoping you might turn out to be a candidate for discretion."

"You are?"

"Yes, Harry. That's why we're having this conversation."

"Oh, yeah? Hey, that's great."

Harry sighed with relief. He didn't know what it was he was saying or doing that was working with her. But he didn't care. Being a candidate for discretion, whatever that was, might be a way back. He'd be a good candidate. He'd show her.

"Run those five principles by me again, please?" He would listen more closely this time. Maybe he could get on her wavelength.

She began: "The first principle is, *Please don't make me wrong, even if you disagree.* Nobody likes to have their worth as a person questioned. They almost always resent it and if they don't get mad, they get even."

"That principle is way off base," he thought to himself. "Everybody knows you have to tell people when they do something wrong, otherwise your business would go down the drain." But he held his tongue. He had agreed to listen to her.

She went on.

"The second principle is, *Hear and understand me.* It is crucially important for people to feel fully listened to and understood. When that has been done, they will be ready to hear what you have to say."

"This principle is just as crazy as the first one," thought Harry. "Imagine me spending my whole day trying to understand some of those numskulls in my refinery." But again he said nothing and listened as she went on.

"The third principle is, *Tell me the truth with compassion.* That means talking *to* people rather than *about* them, and doing it in a respectful and caring rather than a disdainful or condescending way."

"At least that principle seems okay," he said to himself. "I think I can buy into it. I respect people whenever they can prove to me that they deserve it. Besides, I always tell the truth. Everybody knows I tell it like it is." He had managed to filter out the words "with compassion."

"The fourth principle is, *Remember to look for my loving intentions.* That means when someone proposes an idea or a plan, no matter what you think of the plan itself, you explicitly acknowledge that the person has positive reasons—like wanting to help the company— for making their proposal."

"What a load of bull that is!" thought Harry, wanting to pound his fists. "Have I got to mouth this stuff to the goldbrickers back at the refinery if I want her 'discretion'?" he wondered. "What am I getting myself into? This is not going to be easy." But he had promised he would listen to the bitter end.

"The fifth and final principle," continued the Woman, "is, *Acknowledge the greatness within me.* Everyone has the potential to grow, and people will tend to respond positively to anyone who addresses their potential greatness, even if no current evidence of it has yet surfaced."

Then she looked him straight in the eye and said, "Harry, those five principles are what I mean by managing from the heart."

He did not know whether to reveal his honest reaction, wondering if it would kill his chances for this so-called "discretion." He finally decided he might just as well say what he was thinking, since he probably couldn't pull the wool over her eyes.

He walked slowly over to where the Woman was sitting, all 250 impressive pounds of him, and stood above her.

"Ma'am," he began with exaggerated politeness, slowly building in volume and intensity. "You don't know the people I work with. When they leave a valve open that should be shut, they're wrong. That's not an opinion. That's a fact, and there's no way to put a smile on it. When they goof off during working hours and leave the place a mess, what's their loving intention? What's the loving intention behind sheer laziness? When they ask me about my work force at headquarters, I tell them the truth: that they're a sorry bunch of clowns. How would you suggest I compassionately convey that fact to the clowns themselves? And frankly, I don't see any greatness anywhere around me—hell, I'd settle for mediocrity. How can I look for something that's not there? So I really don't see how these principles apply to my situation at all."

By the end of his speech his voice had become calm and confident. When it was over, he gave the Woman a convincing look and sat down.

She smiled, at no one in particular, and shook her head in disbelief. She had known that Harry would not be an easy recruit for managing from the heart and he was more than living up to his reputation. Persuasion wasn't working. She had known it wouldn't. And so, as planned, she proceeded in the language of negotiation and power that he understood so well.

"Harry, let's consider a specific. Your assistant refinery manager, Jim Weiss, came to you with a suggestion for weekly meetings of the top management team. You dismissed the idea as a complete waste of time. Could Jim have had any positive reasons for his suggestion?"

"Not hardly. It was a dumb idea."

The Woman remained seated, calmly exuding a sense of authority to which Harry was unaccustomed. Usually, he was able to ruffle anyone's cool, if he put his mind to it. He had gotten the union's committeemen arguing among themselves the last time they came to him to challenge a decision he had made. He had gotten one of his purchasing directors to confess to taking a kickback from a chemical supplier simply by staring coldly in silence at the man. But this Woman was different. He could see no way to unsettle her.

"Imagine that you and I had a bet for $1,000," she began, "based on whether or not you could come up with a plausible positive intention on Jim's part."

"For a thousand bucks I could probably think of one." He loved to gamble, especially if the bet counted on him to produce the result. "Are you going to pay me a grand if I do?"

"Harry, a thousand dollars would be worthless here. We operate on different currency." She laid her cards on the table. "What if a chance to go back and live your life depended on finding and acknowledging Jim's loving intention?"

"Oh!" His head snapped back, and a light went on in his brain. "I think I see where you're going with this. But I want to be sure. Are you saying that if I agree to try out your five principles, you'll use your 'discretion' and let me go back?"

"Close, but not quite. 'Try out' is not sufficient. To earn 'discretion' you must agree to *live* the five principles, to apply them to all of your relationships, personal and professional. All of them all of the time."

"But what if I screw up and forget?"

"You'll have twenty-four hours to correct any failure."

"And if I miss the deadline?"

"You'll be back here with no more discretion."

"Now, that's one tough deal."

"Harry, it's up to you. You said you could find Jim's loving intention for a thousand dollars. Is it worth it to you to learn to manage using all five principles for another chance to live your life?"

"You have a way of putting things in perspective."

"So, do we have a deal?"

More than anything, he wished there was another way to get back. But it looked like "discretion" was the only flight from here to there, she held the only ticket, and she was naming her price for it.

Inside his head he gave himself the old pep talk: "Harry, you're used to dealing with limit situations. You've had impossible jobs to do in your life before this, many of them for high stakes, and you've made it through. You can pull it off."

He stood up, walked over to the Woman, and shook her hand.

"We have a deal," he said in the voice and the smile he always saved for his best clients. "When do I leave?"

The Woman stood up and smiled a warm smile in return.

"Harry, I think you're going to like it."

"Please don't make me wrong, even if you disagree"

All at once the room began to change. Chairs, walls, the Woman—everything seemed to be shifting, swaying, undulating, and vibrating like heat waves rising off the pavement on a hot summer day. Harry felt dizzy. He was coming to the surface and then sliding back into unconsciousness, again and again. Finally, slowly, he came to.

As his vision focused, he was looking into what seemed the blurred face of a nurse.

"Where am I?" asked Harry, blinking. His words came out slurred and his mouth felt heavy, as if it were full of sludge.

"You are in intensive care and you're going to be just fine, Mr. Hartwell."

The rest of the room slowly came into focus, as he blinked some more. He recognized it as the walls, ceilings, and complex machines of a hospital room.

"What happened? How did I get here?" Harry felt awful, as if a couple of football players were sitting on his chest. He tried to lift his arms, but they felt pinned down.

"You had a mild heart seizure," said the heavyset, middle-aged nurse as she checked his intravenous tubes and the video screen monitoring his heart.

"Where's the Woman I've been talking with?" he asked, his eyes scanning the room in search of her presence.

"You haven't been talking to anyone, Mr. Hartwell. As a matter of fact, you've been unconscious for several hours, and just now came out of it."

"Well, then I must have had a dream that felt so real that I don't think it was a dream."

He could easily picture the Woman, even now. "Nothing like this fat old nurse," he commented to himself.

"Your wife and son have been waiting to see you since this afternoon. They just went down for something to eat. When they get back, I'll bring them in to see you for a few moments. Meantime, get some sleep," said the nurse, her hands resting on the chrome safety bars at the side of his bed. "Your body has been under extreme stress. I'll be back to check up on you and bring your medication. If you need me, my name is Mrs. Covell."

As Harry lay there in the quiet room, his mind struggled to make sense of the dream, or whatever it was, when he had been talking to the Woman about receiving discretionary time and using five principles and having twenty-four hours to correct any mistakes.

"Did it really happen?" he asked himself. He wondered if it was as real as the hospital's distinctive antiseptic smell, or the heart monitor he could hear beeping quietly near his bed, or the intravenous feeding tube he could feel connected to his arm? Was it as real as the hazardous waste disposal contract that waited for him on his desk? Or the whole refinery that he managed?

"The whole damn refinery!" he said aloud, starting a flow of adrenalin in his body. "I've gotta get back there, or talk to someone who can pass orders through about the plot plans and those detailed engineering studies on the new north distillation columns. Where's that nurse? Why isn't someone here to help me get into gear?"

His voice, picked up by a microphone near his bed, came over the emergency monitor at the nurses' station.

"Is something wrong, Mr. Hartwell?" asked the matronly Mrs. Covell hurrying back into his room.

"Hell, yes! I need to get to work."

The nurse replied with a patronizing smile at Harry tied to his bed.

"Great! Now, get me a phone. I've got to get my staff over here right away."

The electronic line on the computer screen monitoring Harry's heart, that had been moving in steady but weak blips, did a hop, skip, and a jump.

The nurse stood at Harry's side in wide-eyed surprise.

"Don't stand there, Mrs. Covell, with your mouth hanging open. I've got a business to run. Profits blow out the window if I don't make decisions before five o'clock today."

Harry tried to sit up, but the nurse's hand went quickly to his shoulder.

"Mr. Hartwell," said the nurse, holding him down, "you're not doing any business today except the business of resting and healing your heart. Remember, you have put your heart under extreme stress and it has taken a toll on your entire system."

Whatever was wrong with his body, Harry's mind was active and it was back in the business groove. Tied to a bed, he could see nothing but big deals and profits evaporating.

"You are one lucky man, Mr. Hartwell. As of now, your heart seems to indicate no extensive or permanent damage."

"I've got a damn good ticker," boasted Harry, pointing toward his heart. Then he remembered it was the only ticker he had, and he felt a momentary scare, which he covered up immediately with a sharp command. "Hand me that phone," he demanded, "like I asked you before, and dial my office. I can't manage it myself with all these confounded wires and tubes you've got me connected to."

"Rest is all you're going to get from me," she replied. "The only business you are allowed to manage in this hospital is the business of your health, and I can tell you right now that you are going to have quite a task doing that."

He looked at her warily from the corner of his eye.

"From now on, first of all," she began counting on her stubby fingers, "you're going to have to cut high-cholesterol foods out of your diet. Completely. Second, steak and all red meats are off your list. No fried foods either. Third, no coffee, no alcohol, no milk products, no sugar. And you're going to have to lose a lot of weight. My guess is the doctor will insist on a strict diet and daily exercise that will help you lose fifty pounds in the next year."

His face turned red. Did this battle-ax of a nurse think she was dealing with Bambi's cousin?

"Don't hand me that garbage, lady," he roared. "Who are you to tell me how to live my life? What do you know? You're only a bedpan changer. Take your guesses about what I can eat and what I can't and stuff them. If you want to meddle in someone's life, carry your bad news somewhere else."

The nurse's body stiffened, she gritted her teeth, and glowered at him. She turned to go.

He said, "Don't spread tacks in front of *my* tires."

As she left the room, she vowed under her breath that this obnoxious man wouldn't hear another kind word from her.

"Too bad some patients have to act like constipated crocodiles," she said aloud to another nurse passing in the corridor.

Back in the room, a cloud of anger, confusion, and fear hovered about Harry. He thought of the Woman in the dream, or whatever that experience was, and what she would have said about the interaction he just had with the nurse. "It had probably violated one of her five principles," he thought.

"You didn't dream me, Harry," came the familiar Woman's voice. "And you just blew it royally with Mrs. Covell."

Harry looked around the room, startled. Although he couldn't see the Woman, he was sure he had heard her voice.

He waited.

"You violated Principle One: *Please don't make me wrong, even if you disagree*," came the voice again.

The voice was somehow inside his head. Unmistakably.

"Remember our deal, Harry. Twenty-four hours to correct a mistake. The clock started ticking as soon as the nurse left the room."

"So, what do I do? What do I do?" asked Harry, looking around the room. It was unnerving to confront someone he couldn't see.

"How do you think she's feeling right now?" asked the Woman. Her voice echoed in Harry's head.

"How should I know?" answered Harry, annoyed that the discretionary Woman wasn't a dream after all. Since it seemed she wasn't going to leave, either, Harry threw her a bone.

"I guess she looked a bit upset when she walked out," he admitted. "I hope she was. She deserved what she got."

"What do you think you said that might have upset her?" the Woman continued.

Harry was quiet. Finally, he sighed. "I guess I might have suggested that she didn't know what she was doing."

"*Might* have suggested, Harry?" the Woman echoed.

"So, what was I supposed to say?"

"It seemed that something she said threatened you."

"What do you mean, 'threatened me'? Nothing threatened me."

"The nurse said you would have to change the way you ate and the way you exercised," the Woman explained calmly. "Because you didn't like the idea of those changes, you felt threatened."

"How is that threatening?" Harry asked. There was an undertone of scorn in his voice, the way a little boy talks to his playmates about not being afraid of lightning, when there's no lightning to test his courage.

"It's threatening because you know that if you don't change, you might have another heart attack. But instead of owning up to feeling threatened or scared, you insulted her."

"Well, maybe I did a bit," he admitted. "So, how do I fix it up?"

"Instead of insulting her again," the Woman suggested, "perhaps you can tell her about your concerns."

"I don't want to change what I eat," asserted Harry. "I enjoy what I eat. I'm not a rabbit. I don't want to become some polyunsaturated wimp. I heard somewhere that just one little aspirin a day would protect these strong American arteries of mine. Why can't I just take an aspirin, or even two, every day? Besides, I don't want to lose fifty pounds. I like what I weigh." Harry paused for breath, a momentary pain in his lungs reminding him of his mortality. "But, if I don't change, it'll kill me. I know enough guys like me who overdid it and kicked the bucket. I'm not ready to go over the rainbow yet."

"All that's fine to say to the nurse, Harry. That wouldn't insult her."

"So, you're telling me that it's all right to talk about my sour reactions to the things she said?"

"That's certainly preferable to being referred to as a bedpan changer."

"I don't remember clearly all those rules you laid down when I was in a coma. Give me some help."

"When someone like the nurse comes to you," began the Woman reassuringly, "remember that an unspoken request they make of you is: *Please don't make me wrong*. You can still have reactions. You can talk about your feelings and concerns, but let your words be about you and how you are taking the situation. So, if you're feeling shell-shocked, say it. Don't turn your feelings of being threatened into a threatening attack on her. What is offensive and unacceptable to her is when you brand her with negative labels like 'meddling.' Instead, tell her about yourself."

"How do I do that?" He was annoyed that on top of dealing with all the pain, the tubes, and monitors on his body, he had to learn a new lesson in how to behave toward others.

"Start your sentences with the word 'I,'" began the Woman, "and finish them by describing yourself, your state of mind, your feelings, your wishes. The other person can then take your statements or leave them. The important thing is to make sure that what you say is not insulting. Statements about yourself don't create enemies or bad will. They won't make the nurse shrivel up inside and drive her out of your room."

"I guess you're right. I guess I really screwed it up. So, what do I do to fix things?" As a practical afterthought, he added, "I surely don't want her angry at me and messing up my medication."

"Next time you see her, tell her what you were feeling, and redo the scene."

"I'll try," he replied, closing his eyes.

The real truth was that he wished the Woman would feel an immediate need for a coffee break and vanish from inside his head.

———————◆◆◆———————

At that moment, the door swung open and in walked the same nurse, carrying a tray with his medication. The look on her face, like that of a seasoned infantryman, showed she was ready to sustain another salvo of fire from enemy guns.

"Just tell her," the Woman's voice inside his head coached him, "what *you* were feeling when she told you about your new diet and losing fifty pounds. Restate the situation that upset you and the impact it had on you."

As the nurse handed him the medication, Harry said, "Thank you."

Then he plunged into it.

"Mrs. Covell, when you told me I'd have to cut out cholesterol and have to go on a diet and exercise in order to cut my weight down to 200, I was afraid I'd have to give up a lot of things I really enjoy, like a daily snort of Chivas Regal and an occasional platter of greasy nachos coated with melted cheddar. I mean, I was afraid I couldn't change. And *that* felt very threatening. Either I couldn't change or wouldn't like changing. And I resented being pinned in a corner like that. That's why you got that barbarian reaction from me before. I'd like to apologize."

"I can understand that, Mr. Hartwell," the nurse responded, surprised at the total reversal of his manner. "Lots of people have to do what you'll have to do to stay healthy, and almost everybody finds the announcement of it hard to take. But they find a way. And you seem like a very strong person. I'm sure you can do it." She punctuated her encouragement with a smile.

With that, she whisked out of the room to tend to other tasks.

———◆◆◆◆———

"That was pretty easy," said Harry to the Woman, as if she had been sitting in the green visitor's chair near his bed. The reality was she seemed to have taken up residence inside his head, or his heart, and he could be in touch with her at will.

"That nurse could really handle it," he said, still surprised that he could express his feelings to another human being without brandishing his verbal sword. "She didn't make fun of me for feeling threatened or afraid, as I thought she would. She didn't belittle me. That was terrific."

"In fact, she was very supportive," added the Woman.

"But anyone at my refinery would have had a field day dragging me around the court, if I had apologized to them like that."

"I'm not so sure of that, Harry. When you don't make people wrong, and simply tell them what's happening inside you, the door is then open for them to support you. Instead of making an enemy of the nurse with further scorn and ridicule, you made a friend."

"Do I really scorn and ridicule people at work?"

"I'm afraid you do, almost every chance you get. You love to make people wrong, to lay the blame and rub it in. You do it so universally, Harry, that sometimes you even make your own wife wrong, the person you love most in the world."

"What do you mean?" he retorted indignantly. "I would never put Molly down."

"Sure you would. And you do. Remember last month, the master bathroom for the new addition to your house? You came home from work, and Molly told you the plumber had asked if she wanted a regular bathtub in white."

"Yes," he said shaking his head in disbelief as his memory replayed the scene. "She told the plumber 'yes' when she should have known better. She knew I wanted a tub that was neither white nor regular, but bone-colored and a setup that could be used for both steam and jacuzzi."

"But what did you say to her?" the Woman insisted. "How did you put it?"

"I don't know," he said, as if it were an insult to ask him to remember the exact words he used. "I probably reminded her that we had talked about the tub and thought we had a clear agreement on it."

"True, that was your general intent," the Woman conceded. "But do you remember how you made your point?"

"Well, not precisely," he admitted. "Are you telling me I did some mudslinging at her?"

"Exactly. You taunted her with 'How come you forgot it?' and 'I thought we had an agreement!' and 'Can't you remember anything?' and 'How many times do I have to tell you something?' and 'Next time I'll put it in writing!' and 'Molly the Muffinhead.' You never let her up for air, Harry, all night long and next morning at breakfast. You made her indelibly wrong. You got your precious tub, but every time your wife steps into it now, she has a momentary twinge remembering that day you made her wrong."

"Well, I guess I went a bit overboard," he acknowledged. "But what else could I have said to her? I was really disappointed and angry about that tub."

"Right, Harry. And that's what you could have said to her: 'Molly, I'll be very disappointed and angry if I don't get the tub of my dreams, so please call the plumber and change the order.'"

"Well, now that you put it that way, I can see that there was an alternative approach. I didn't have to stomp her head with her mistake."

"That's right. When people make mistakes, give them a chance to correct the mistake without making the person wrong. Your wife made a mistake with the tub. But instead of looking for a way to get the mistake corrected, you turned *her* into a mistake."

"It was the tub that was wrong, not her?" Harry asked, wanting to make sure he understood.

"Precisely." The Woman paused to let Harry's awareness sink in. Then, she began again. "You also made Molly wrong the time she ordered untreated wood for the deck off the dining room, and again the time she withdrew a big chunk of your joint bank account without telling you and you wrote a check that bounced."

"You've got to admit that both of those were stupid mistakes and she wasn't using her brain."

"And you called her all kinds of names and suggested that she had unscrewed her head and left it in the pantry."

"But she *was* wrong. You've gotta admit that. She was dead wrong."

"You're doing it again, Harry. You're making her wrong. What she mistakenly did doesn't mean that *she* was the mistake. It was the action that was wrong, not Molly herself. That's what this principle means: Call the *mistake* wrong, but please don't make *me* wrong, even if you disagree."

"I've got it," said Harry confidently. "I won't mess up again."

"Changing behavior toward your wife may be one of the most difficult things for you to do," countered the Woman. "You're going to be tested with her, but not tonight. You've had enough for one day."

A̲t the same moment, Molly and Bob, their son, came into the room.

"The whole family!" Harry's face broke into a smile.

"I'm so glad you're okay, darling." She sobbed with relief as she bent over to kiss him. The skin around her eyes was puffed from crying. "I prayed and prayed all afternoon that you would be all right."

"It seems I've been awarded some discretionary time from above today, and I'll be happy to enjoy it with the two of you."

"I called Bob at his dorm this afternoon as soon as I arrived at the hospital," she explained, as Bob came over to touch his father's hand in greeting, "but his roommate said he was on his way home already."

"Did my office call you, Bob?"

"No, dad. I was planning to come home for the weekend anyway. I left right after my last class at noon. But I never expected to find you in the hospital."

"I hadn't planned on it either. In fact, I hadn't planned for a number of things that happened to me today."

At this point, Mrs. Covell came in and asked Molly and Bob to leave.

"I'm sorry, visiting hours are over. You may come back tomorrow. Mr. Hartwell will be feeling better then, but he needs a lot of rest tonight. He and I have been through a lot together today." She cast a wary glance at her patient, wondering whether at this moment he would be acting like Jekyll or Hyde.

"Don't worry, dear," Harry assured his wife. "Mrs. Covell has been taking excellent care of me. In more ways than one, I'm in good hands."

A few days later, on one of her regular visits, an effervescent Molly swept into Harry's hospital room with her usual flurry of excitement and smiles, plus packages from a recent shopping spree. Tall and freckled, with her hair in an upsweep, she looked young for her age. Dropping her packages near the door, she pulled the green chair close to his bed and sat down.

"Well, I did it, Harry!" A big smile spread across her face. "I closed on the Webster's house, the big property on Maple Street that's been listed for almost a year. I know I've mentioned it to you before. Today we met at the lawyer's office and they signed the papers. It'll be the grandest commission I ever made!"

"Nice going, Molly," he said. "You worked hard for it."

He opened his arms to welcome her. "I'm glad you're here."

She leaned over and kissed him, her trim body and young face radiating happiness. Harry and Molly were well-matched. Both of them were witty, bright, and savvy.

"What's with all the packages?" he asked, looking at the shopping bags.

"They're to celebrate my commission and your good news."

"What good news?"

"'Guarded optimism' is what Dr. Stuart said about you when I called him at home last night. 'Lots of rest for him on next month's calendar,'" she added in a tone that mimicked the old doctor. "I predict a rosy future for you, Harry Hartwell."

He laughed at her imitating the old doctor who had cared for the Hartwell family ever since he could remember.

Then Molly said, "By the way, Harry, since you were here in the hospital, I went ahead and mailed the check for Bob's second-semester tuition at college."

"How did he score in his first-semester grades?" he asked. "Did we get his report?"

"Yes, and it was disappointing," Molly admitted hesitantly. "Bob got only a 2.25 grade point average."

When Bob entered college, Harry had agreed to pay his expenses, without question, for the first two years. During his freshman and sophomore years, Bob had shown himself to be a disappointingly average student, attaining only a 2.0 out of 4.0. Harry remembered that Bob's SAT scores in high school showed he was capable of doing much better than average, so before the fall semester of his junior year began, in the presence of Molly, Harry had said to him, "If you want your mother and me to keep paying your college tuition, you'll have to get a 2.5. If you slip below that, you'll be on your own financially. Your mother agrees with this proposal," to which Molly had nodded. "But is it acceptable to you?" Harry asked his son. Bob had confidently replied, "Sure, dad, I can manage that." And that was their agreement.

But Bob hadn't managed it, as Molly had just acknowledged.

Harry took a moment to digest the news, and then he blew up.

"What! He got 2.25 and you paid his tuition? What the hell did you do that for? You are dumb, Molly. Dumb, dumb, dumb! You paid it, and you knew darn well that our deal with him was, if he didn't get at least a 2.5 we would cut off his tuition, and let him fend for himself!" Beads of sweat began to appear on his forehead.

"Calm down, Harry. I remember what we said, and I thought about it. You were sick and I didn't want to bother you, and it felt cruel to cut off our own son's college education in the middle of the school year. Besides, Bob promised he would do better."

"Good old Molly! Good old bleeding heart!" Harry slapped his head. "You're teaching him to be a con artist. Damn, Molly, he's never going to learn to be responsible. He knew you were a soft touch."

"He promised he'd do better." She emphasized each word.

"Promises!" he shouted. "Promises are worth zilch. Performance is the bottom line. If I treated our employees the way you coddle our son, we wouldn't produce any fuel."

"And if I talked to you the way you're talking to me right now, Harry Hartwell, I don't think you'd appreciate it. I certainly don't, and I'll bet your employees don't either."

He said nothing, and she continued with controlled anger. "When Bob takes a job at your refinery, then you'll be his boss. At the moment, however, you are merely his father. Remember that, please, and treat him as your flesh and blood, not as your hired hand."

At that moment the nurse came in to administer some treatment, so Molly stood up to take her leave.

She gave him a perfunctory departing kiss.

———————————◆◈◆———————————

"Harry," came the familiar Woman's voice, as soon as the nurse left the room. "You did it again. You made Molly wrong."

"Well, I had no choice," said Harry sheepishly.

"The clock just started ticking again. What are you going to do?"

"Wait a minute," countered Harry. Pointing an accusing finger at no one in particular, he added, "You've got to admit she was wrong to pay that tuition. After all, it went against our agreement with Bob. As an adult, he's got to fulfill his side of the agreement, if we're going to be faithful to our side. I feel cheated by him. He knew the score. It was all out in the open. I wasn't hiding anything up my sleeve. I want the best for my son, and letting him manipulate Molly is no good for him or her. He's the punk who pulled a fast one, and, thanks to Molly, got away with it. I have every right to feel angry and cheated, don't I?"

"Sure you do, Harry. But that's not the message you communicated to Molly. She became your scapegoat. You called her names. You spent all your energy making *her* wrong. And you almost gave yourself another heart seizure along with it."

Harry pondered this for a moment.

"Do you think I can clean it up with a phone call?"

"I'm sure Molly would appreciate any sincere gesture from you."

"But what do I say?" he asked. "I still think she was dead wrong to have written that check."

"Harry, she's already gotten *that* message from you. There's not a shadow of doubt in her mind that you strongly disapproved of what she did. Could you, instead, tell her about your anger at feeling cheated by Bob, without having to make her or him wrong?"

"Well, tact doesn't seem to be my strong suit. I think I'm better at just squashing others and the hell with it."

"I'm not surprised," replied the Woman. "Most people who have the habit of blaming, criticizing, accusing or using other ways of making people wrong have a hard time shifting their behavior. Old habits, especially destructive ones, mightily resist dying. Don't expect to be an expert in Principle One overnight."

Later, after some rehearsal with the Woman, he called Molly to apologize.

"I'm sorry, old girl, for blowing up at you the way I did. I was angry at Bob and I took it out on you."

"That's okay, Harry. You're under a lot of stress right now. Like you, I was disappointed when I heard about Bob's low grades."

"And I felt betrayed by his choosing to manipulate you rather than be an adult and acknowledge to us that he had not kept his part of the deal."

"I'm angry, too."

"There wasn't any good reason for those low grades, was there? I mean, he hasn't been sick, has he?"

"Not as far as I can tell," Molly sighed. "He gave me the usual excuses—a busy social life, extra curricular things, late with term papers, always waiting till the last minute to do assignments, and often not getting them in on time, and so on."

"I sort of wish you had never told me about sending the tuition check."

"I hadn't planned to, Harry. Really. And I certainly didn't bring the matter up to upset you. Mainly, I wanted to get out some of my own anger and guilt."

"The truth is, we were both angry and disappointed."

Harry hung up the phone, feeling good about Molly's reaction and secretly pleased with himself for having outsmarted the discretionary clock once again.

"You came through that one well enough, Harry," said the Woman, "though for a minute I thought you were going to slip back into blaming her for Bob's poor grades."

"A few times," Harry admitted, "I could feel accusations almost forming on my lips, but I remembered the clock. Amazing how a ticking clock can get my attention."

A few days later, Hector Morales, head of purchasing at Harry's Ramoco refinery, came into the hospital room, his dark eyes all smiles. Short and stocky, Hector was a young, warm-hearted guy—sometimes even thoughtful. For example, instead of the usual flowers or the old-fashioned box of candy, he brought a book of political cartoons by Herblock, Harry's favorite cartoonist. Herblock would love to caricature a pair like Harry and Hector: the overbearing boss and his scheming money man. An accountant by training, Hector was no mere numbers cruncher, but an ambitious and creative idea man, always coming up with new angles.

Adjusting his tie and tugging his suit coat to make sure it hung just right, Hector walked right up to Harry's bedside. He liked being close to people when he spoke to them. After the usual preliminaries of "How are you feeling, Harry?" and "Are you following doctor's orders?" and "I hope you're taking good care of yourself," Hector gently shifted the theme into "We miss you at the refinery." and "Your chair is getting dusty." Soon, he was excitedly spilling the proposal that had brought him to Harry's bedside.

"Harry, I'm sorry to bother you at a time like this, but Ramoco has a big opportunity and our refinery can grab it."

"Yeah? A big feather in our cap?" said Harry, intrigued. "What is it?"

Hector leaned closer. "I heard a rumor," continued Morales softly, as if a competitor's ear was listening behind the closed door, "that the Saudis are going to dump a lot of oil. Cheap. As much as four dollars per barrel off the current OPEC prices. We need to be ready to buy it."

"You're full of it, Morales!" said Harry sharply, dismissing his subordinate. "Get out of here. That rumor is pure craziness. Do you think, because I'm lying in a hospital bed, that my brain's in a cocoon?"

Hector stepped back and looked at Harry in silence, his hands hanging limply at his sides.

"Did you notice what you just did, Harry?" interrupted the inner voice of the Woman. "You made Hector wrong."

"Damn!" said Harry, sincerely regretting his critical outburst.

Hector, unaware of the dialogue going on with the Woman, thought Harry's comment was meant for him, and turned to leave.

"Maybe, before he goes," the Woman added, "you can save the situation. Quick, how did you *feel* when he told you about the Saudis dumping oil on the open market?"

"I didn't believe the rumor," replied Harry silently. "That's what I told him."

"There's a big difference in saying, 'You're full of it.' and, 'I don't believe the rumor,'" she replied. "So, would you now tell Hector what you really felt, so you can hear what he has to say without biting off his head."

"Hector," Harry called loudly but apologetically, "come back here. I didn't mean to chew your head off just now. What I meant to say was that I find it hard to swallow that rumor. I'm having trouble believing that the Saudis would do something *that* dumb—to cut off their nose to spite their face."

Hector turned and faced Harry's bed.

"Me, too, boss," he said gently, relieved to see Harry smiling. And pointing his fingers at his own chest, the younger man said, "But I checked it out through our usual Mideast channels, and it seems to be on the level. The Saudis are finally fed up with the other OPEC countries all cheating on their quotas. So, as a way of getting the others in line, the Saudis plan to create a lot of financial pain and punishment by dumping oil."

"You mean they're using this tactic as a way of disciplining the other OPECs to toe the line?" Harry still found it hard to digest the rumor.

"It looks like that," replied Hector. "And what it looks like from our perspective is that we have a short-term opportunity for stocking up on some cheap crude."

"That's very clever of you, Hector." Harry was beginning to see the logic behind the rumor. "Thanks for being on the ball," he said with genuine gratitude.

"So, boss," said Hector eagerly sliding into his main point, "I would like your authorization to go beyond our normal inventory limit for this one-time spot purchase."

It occurred to Harry to say: "If this play doesn't work out the way you drew the picture, Morales, you're in for it. If that price goes down further or, worse, stays down, your ass is grass." But he restrained himself.

"I'm glad you didn't say what surfaced in your mind a moment ago," the Woman's smiling approval sounded inside him. "There's no need to state the obvious in a punitive way. Hector knows the risks involved as well as you do. There is only one issue here: Do you want to take the risk and put yourself on the line, or not?"

"Go ahead, Hector," said Harry aloud. "I'll authorize it."

"Thanks, boss. It's gonna' work out great. Don't you worry. By the way, when are you coming back? We really miss you."

"Probably in a couple of weeks," said Harry. "The doc said I had a fighter's body and the old pump will heal fast. I can't wait to get back on the field. I'm not cut out for the sidelines."

"Great, boss," said Hector, as he looked back from the door. "I'll tell everybody you'll be back in no time."

———— ◆•◆•◆ ————

"Harry, I'm proud of you," said the Woman. "Aside from your opening comment to Hector's proposal, making him wrong, you carried on superbly, with little need for coaching from me."

"I never realized how quick I am to jump to conclusions and bring the axe down on people," explained Harry, almost surprised at his growing awareness of how judgmentally he normally behaved toward others.

"The thing to remember is, when you make people wrong, you set yourself up as right. When you say to someone, 'You're dumb,' you also say, 'But I'm smart.' Or, if you call someone 'lazy,' the implication is, 'I'm hardworking and, thank God, I am not like you.'"

"My old man always wanted me to be better than my classmates," said Harry. "'I want the trophy sitting in *my* house' is what he used to say."

"Your father also probably taught you that the only way to win was to make the other guy lose."

"That's right," replied Harry. "What other way is there?"

"There are ways to win without making others lose. Some people feel that they have really won only if they cut off the other guy's head. You would have kicked Morales out the door with your harsh comments, if you hadn't redeemed yourself and stopped making him wrong."

"I guess I'm a real put-down artist," he said, adding, "Secretly, I'm kind of proud of my masterful barbs."

"Well, some of the put-down statements you have been making are rather heartless. They can push people away. They express coldness and distance. They can put up walls between you and others. Basically, they say to the other person, 'I want no part of you.' And because they are threatening and bullying, they seldom produce willing cooperation."

"I have sort of noticed that." His head gave a slow nod.

"But as soon as you told the nurse, your wife, and Morales what was going on inside you, they put down their defenses. They knew you were not about to send their self-esteem through a shredder."

"I just have this incredible drive to come out on top, to be the winner."

"That's great, as long as you remember that everyone else would like much the same thing for themselves. In your zeal to get the job done, you can easily fall into the habit of making others wrong, making them the losers. But on a real team, all members stick together; they either all win or they all lose. On a real team, you can't afford to bash and blame the other players, because that creates mistrust and undermines the team relationship. Harry, everybody in the refinery needs to be able to count on you supporting them, especially since you're their manager."

"I can see that makes sense. But what about productivity? That's the bottom line of my job. How does not making people wrong impact on productivity?"

"It's very simple. People are more productive and perform at their best when they feel good about themselves and when they feel good about what they do. It's impossible for individuals to feel really good about themselves and what they're doing if they are constantly being told they are wrong. To be productive, people need to be told what they're doing that's right and how their work is making a worthwhile contribution to something. People like to be told they are a contributing part of a winning team."

"I never heard it put so clearly before," he said.

"Making everybody a winner works outside the refinery, too," she continued. "When you work with suppliers and customers, make them feel right also. Don't undermine any relationship."

"But how do you do it when people are really wrong—excuse me, when people *do* something really wrong? What do you say?" Harry was genuinely interested.

"Take some of your familiar 'make wrong' statements and turn them around," explained the Woman. "On the one hand, some of your standard comments include: 'You're blind and out in left field,' or, 'You're just leading us off the track,' or, 'You just stupidly missed the point I was trying to make,' or, 'Now, there's a comment that is useless.' On the other hand, you could try affirming the parts of their behavior that are helpful, such as, 'That question you just asked sheds a new light on the problem,' or, 'A part of the point you just made will contribute to the solution,' or, 'What you just said emphasizes an important, but often overlooked, point,' or, turning to others at a meeting and asking, 'How can we use that observation Bill just made?' or, 'It's nice to know you are thinking on behalf of the team.'"

"The first set of comments you just presented sound very familiar to me. I find it easy to make cracks like that," admitted Harry. "But the other comments are really 'not me.' Coming out of my mouth they feel phony."

"Initial awkwardness is natural, Harry," said the Woman. "It's very normal when learning new habits. That's what the discretionary period is all about, learning new habits of the heart. You're struggling, but you're also learning to do it right. I trust you'll do as well with the second principle."

"Hear And Understand Me"

With a satisfied grin, Harry gently eased himself into the leather chair behind his own desk. Savoring his first moments back at Ramoco, he recognized the familiar petroleum scents of the refinery.

"Pure oxygen to energize my business lungs," he thought, taking a deep breath.

At home, he had been chafing at the bit, driving Molly crazy, snapping at the doctor. Finally, after only three weeks of confinement, he got them to open the corral and set him free.

"Only half-days for a while," cautioned Dr. Stuart, "until your strength builds up again."

Harry had come to the office early, long before his staff would be in to make a fuss over him. He wanted to be alone for a while, just to experience what it felt like to be sitting in his chair again, able to spin around and look out the window at the innards of the refinery. With deep satisfaction, he gazed at the complex maze of pipes connecting the distillation columns and catalytic cracking units that were required to produce the many refined oils, solvents, fuels, and petrochemicals at Ramoco. He realized how much he had missed calling the shots, being in control of operations.

A cup of herbal tea sat on the desk before him. He found its taste disappointing. During the past three weeks at home, he had tried all the flavors—lemon, orange, mint, raspberry, blackberry, strawberry, almond—but none of them scored with him the way a steaming cup of hot coffee did. However, for him, or so the doctor said, coffee was off limits.

"If my nostrils as much as bend over to sniff the aroma of your coffee, darling" he had told Molly, when the order to lay off coffee had been put into his Rule Book, "you should throw a flag on the play, like a good referee, and penalize me an extra quarter of a mile on my morning walk."

So far, there had been no penalties. Applying his customary discipline and will-power, Harry stuck to his assigned diet and walks. He was the kind of person who, when he put his mind to something, made it happen.

He was also pleased to discover that he was one for whom an aspirin a day was recommended. Anything that raised his percentages for a longer life gave him great pleasure.

Molly had suggested he keep a Progress Chart to track his weight improvement, and he verbally rewarded her with a "promotion" for the idea. At least he hadn't made her wrong. Sitting at his desk in the quiet office, he decided that designing such a chart would be the first assignment he would give his Administrative Assistant Ann Laney. That way, he could keep score of his health game, day by day.

———◆◆◆———

During his convalescence at home, the Woman hadn't left the scene, much as Harry would have hoped at the beginning. She wasn't a figment of his imagination. Rather, she had become a permanent fixture in his consciousness. He had only to think a message or a question to her, and he would clearly hear her voice in his mind.

At other times, she would be first to make her presence known or be the one to initiate a dialogue. Usually, it was to make him aware that he had said something to set the discretionary clock ticking again.

All in all, though, his batting average was pretty good.

At home, the Woman continued to coach Harry on the five principles of managing from the heart. She reminded him that the second principle, *Hear and understand me,* would probably prove troublesome to him.

"Something has been bothering me about your second principle," he said, sitting on a rocking chair near the desk in his study. He had been looking at a photograph of his father and himself as a college student standing in front of the Ramoco refinery.

"Tell me about it," the Woman replied.

"I can see how this principle, if practiced, might make people feel good, but how about productivity? My father used to say, 'Productivity is the only principle in the oil business.' And that's the way I've been running my refinery."

"And your concern is that productivity is not even on the list of principles for managing from the heart."

"That's exactly my point," he said. "How do I square having a productive operation with a 'Hear and understand me' mentality?"

"You're saying that as a Ramoco manager it's not enough that the five principles are nice and humane and make people feel good. That's not a strong enough reason to put them into practice."

"If you want the real truth," he said, after a pause, "I'm doing all this stuff only because I'm on discretion. I don't really see how you and your principles can help me do my real job as a refinery manager. I'm talking about productivity, the bottom line."

"I'm glad you want to get to the bottom line, Harry. I can see that productivity is most important to you."

"Right. 'Produce or Die!' That's where it's at in this business."

"And here I am telling you, 'Manage from the heart or die!' To you, those two ultimatums seem to be in conflict."

"They sure are," he said, opening his hand in a gesture of agreement. "I mean, because of you, I have to manage from the heart, but the people I work with don't. That sets up an immediate conflict. But even if every manager in my refinery began practicing these five principles, would we really be more effective?"

"And when you say 'effective' you don't mean 'nice and sweet,' you mean being a productive refinery. You wouldn't consider seriously any management plan that wouldn't help your people be more productive."

"Precisely," he said. "I couldn't have put it better myself."

"For now, let's just stay with the second principle, Harry, *Hear and understand me.*"

"Okay," he agreed. "Don't get me wrong. I think listening to what other people have to say is a good idea in general. But I've got a big responsibility to keep a major oil refinery working. Show me how Principle Two affects productivity."

"When are people most productive in your refinery, Harry?"

He didn't hesitate a moment. "When they know what they're supposed to do and they do it." He was repeating something he had heard his father say a thousand times.

"Compared to machines," she asked him, "how long do you think people can go on doing what they're supposed to be doing without having some feelings, thoughts, and ideas about their work?"

"Theoretically, machines can go on for ten to twenty years or more with normal lubrication and maintenance, I guess, but people need to talk. Heaven knows, I can attest to that. I have to listen to people all day long."

"That's right. People need to say how they're feeling, to share their thoughts, to be appreciated and valued."

"So, even when my employees just want to dump their emotional garbage, I should be willing to listen to them and try to understand them?"

"That's one good way you could help make them feel good about themselves. When you listen and understand, it makes them feel they are important to the refinery and that they're making a contribution."

"Sort of like putting oil and grease on the machines to make them work more smoothly?" he asked.

"Not quite," the Woman clarified. "Machines don't have hearts and feelings. They don't have dreams and hopes the way you and I do. People need to know that they are an important part of what goes on in your refinery, and listening and understanding helps make them feel connected to you and to what's important to you, which in this case is the refinery's productivity."

"So," he asked, "your point is that listening helps my employees feel good about themselves and their work, and that makes them productive?"

"Right. I think it is very difficult for people to feel important and think they are making a contribution, if no one really hears and understands what they are saying."

"I never thought about it that way, but it makes sense." Harry got up from the rocking chair. "I'll go along with you for now, but I still have reservations."

"Why are you willing to go along, Harry, even though you have reservations?"

Harry had to think about that question. Finally, he smiled and said, "Let's just say I think you've been hearing and understanding me."

———————◆•◆•◆———————

A few days later, on a morning when the ground was wet after a night's rainfall, while Harry was doing his jaunt through the wooded park near his home, the Woman's voice began, "Are you ready to review the application of Principle Two?"

Harry nodded his assent. He also picked up his stride.

He had come to enjoy the Woman's company, even though she never physically appeared. When he was alone, he liked to talk aloud to her. He sometimes pictured her walking by his side in her long robe, the way he remembered her in the shiny white room. Somehow it felt more natural to him that way.

She began her lesson gently.

"We all want to be heard and understood, Harry. Unfortunately, it rarely happens. So few people really listen."

"I know what you mean," he said, turning his head as if to look at her.

"I pride myself on being a good listener," he continued. "My subordinates all know they can't snow me or pull the wool over my eyes."

"I'm talking about more than just getting facts straight," she corrected. "I mean really understanding other people in the way they intend to be understood. Poor listening and misunderstanding have wrecked many a relationship and cost organizations untold millions."

"That's exactly what I tell my rank and file," he agreed. "Getting things wrong costs big bucks. My people know they'd better have the facts straight because I listen carefully and ask a lot of questions. And when I ask, I want answers. There's no whining and skirting the issue when they talk to me."

"Sometimes you really don't listen at all, Harry, despite your protestations."

"What do you mean?" he asked defensively.

The Woman was silent for a moment.

He stopped and turned his body as if to confront her.

"Let's go back to a management committee meeting about a year ago," the Woman began. "Connie Marucca, corporate V.P. for Marketing and Sales, expressed a concern about quality control with Ramoco's heating oil. Almost before she could finish making her point, do you remember how you verbally dumped all over her?"

Harry remembered: He had jumped up from his seat at the head of the boardroom table, shouting, "I would like to respond to that accusation. First of all, Connie, you do not know what you are talking about. Second, we have had very few customer complaints about quality. Third, all the variances on the reports from Operations are within normal limits. Fourth, aside from your being Ramoco's resident paranoid, I think you're using this heating oil quality issue maliciously, as a way of reviving the union's objection to a statistical quality control system."

"You'll also remember," said the Woman, "Connie went out of that meeting feeling beaten up and unheard. As a result, within six months, three electrical power companies cancelled their heating oil contracts with Ramoco and you lost three major accounts, all of whom had been valued clients for years."

Harry snorted. "I remember vividly when word came in about those cancellations," he said. "I called an emergency meeting of the management committee. I was so angry at Connie for letting those accounts slip through her fingers that I almost tried to get her canned."

"But you didn't," interposed the Woman, "because, in her tears, she said to you, 'I finally got your attention, Harry, about the need for quality control in our heating oils. You would never listen.' And you finally heard what she was saying. Those customers dropped Ramoco for precisely the reason Connie had warned about, quality that was not sufficiently consistent to meet customer demands. Had she been heard and understood in the first place, the business loss might have been averted."

"She should have given us some advance notice, shown us specific data to prove her point," insisted Harry weakly.

"She tried to, but your mind was closed. First, you wouldn't listen. And, second, when Ramoco lost, you tried to make *her* wrong."

Already, Harry had two strikes against him. He had swung and missed Principle One as well as Principle Two.

"I thought I at least had Principle Two down pat," he said, dejected. "But it seems I'm not seeing something."

"There is an old saying that goes, 'Why is there never enough time to do it right, but always enough time to do it over?' Poor listening often guarantees that the job will have to be done over."

"So, let's replay the scene with Connie," suggested Harry. "How could I have done a better job of listening? I thought I understood what she was saying at that first meeting. After all, I do know the oil business better than she does."

"Harry, the message you often communicate to people at Ramoco is: 'Don't confuse me with the facts, I already have an opinion.' That's why you get so few suggestions. People don't have your trust. What they usually say to themselves is: 'Harry never lets you finish because he's sure he already knows what you're going to say' or 'Harry doesn't want your information since he already knows what the answer is.'"

"You sure know how to hurt a guy," he said, almost stepping into a puddle left over from last night's rain. He angrily kicked a twig lying on his path. "I'd switch your channel off," he said, "if I didn't know this was a matter of life and death."

"I'm here to help you stay alive, Harry," came the Woman's voice. "I'm on your side. Either we both win or neither of us wins."

"Okay," he conceded. "It's hard to listen to you say these things about me. I had no idea that's how people saw me. I always thought I was a good listener and understood clearly what people said to me."

"You may often think you understand what someone is saying, but to make sure, you need to check it out. Give others the chance to express themselves. Sometimes they have good ideas. If, at that first meeting, you had given Connie a chance to bring out all her facts and then reflected back your sense of what she was trying to say, the meeting might have moved from the merits of new quality control procedures, to the existing marketing situation, and to the implications for new business. Instead of losing contracts, you could have designed ways to increase profits that morning."

"Are you telling me I should hear people out fully before responding, is that it?"

"That's a big part of it, Harry. It's also important during the early part of a discussion to *reply to people by summarizing your understanding of what they just said.* This is what is called a Listening Check. It gives evidence that the person has been heard and offers the person an opportunity to clear up any misunderstandings."

"Don't you think it's a waste of time to parrot back to people what they've just said to you?"

"Listening is not a passive skill, Harry," she explained. "If you paraphrase back to people the gist of what they've just said to you—in a Listening Check—it tells them that you've gotten their message. It also assures them that you're really listening."

"That would drive me crazy, always telling people what they've just said to me. Besides, I would sound stupid doing it."

"No, you wouldn't. First of all, you don't have to give a verbal replay after every sentence. That _would_ annoy people. But, from time to time, if you paraphrase what others say to you, you remind them that you are listening and trying to understand. And if you've missed some important point they were trying to make, this would give them a chance to clarify their meaning. For example, a few moments ago you missed my point about reflecting back what people say, and when you gave me feedback it allowed me to clarify what I wanted to say."

"It also proved that I was trying to listen," he said. He hoped this small victory would show that he was tracking with Principle Two.

"Yes, it did," she agreed, "and it also enabled you to gain my trust, so I am willing and eager to keep communicating with you."

"I'm a captive audience," said Harry with a wry smile.

"These principles of managing from the heart also apply to personal issues as well," she said. "When you listen actively, you listen primarily for content, for information, for ideas. But you also listen for attitudes, intentions, and feelings. Information often comes packaged in an important feeling."

"What do attitudes and feelings have to do with running an oil refinery?" he asked, still convinced that personal feelings were an interference in the workplace. "My business is based on hard facts and reliable information, not any of that soft stuff. You can't manufacture marketable products out of emotions. It's a different game entirely." Harry sensed the Woman did not agree.

"Remember when you visited Dan Harwood, your manager on the night shift, in April?"

" Yes, " he replied cautiously. "What are you driving at?"

"Can you replay the scene?"

"I suppose if I don't do it, you will."

It was about an hour and a half into the night shift on a quiet April evening. Harry had been working late and, before he drove home, he decided to do a walk-through inspection of the refinery. He believed a general manager ought to know firsthand what was going on in his refinery.

On his way down the corridor, he passed by Dan's office. Through the glass, he could see Dan hunched over at his desk, holding his head in his hands. "Probably trying to figure out a solution to a problem," Harry thought. Ten minutes later, after the walk-through and on his way back to his office to pick up his coat and briefcase, he looked in again on Dan. He was still in the same position, head in his hands. "Funny," Harry said to himself.

He tapped on the glass to get Dan's attention. Dan slowly looked up. Startled to see Harry at his door, he hurried to open it. His eyes were red-rimmed and bloodshot.

"Didn't mean to disturb you, Dan. You seemed lost in thought. Is everything all right?"

"I haven't been feeling well lately," explained Dan, his hand still on the doorknob. "I'm a little down, I guess."

"Yes, I know. Everyone's been fighting colds. I hope you're taking something for it."

"I am, but nothing seems to be working."

Harry turned and pointed toward the solvents unit. "Say, has everyone shown up on your shift? I was walking down there a few minutes ago, and it seemed you didn't have a full complement."

"Well, I think so."

"What do you mean, 'think so'?"

"Well, I haven't been down there yet."

"What are you doing up here, then?" Harry was startled. "Your shift has been on for nearly two hours. You can't simply assume everything is going smoothly down there. Come on, Dan, let's get with it."

"I was just about to go down when you came by," he said defensively.

"I hope so. You had been sitting in here with your head in your hands for the past ten minutes, at least. Look, if you need a day of sick leave to take care of that cold, do it. But when you show up here, you've got to run your shift."

Harry moved out of the doorway to let Dan pass.

"You're right, Harry." He stepped out into the corridor.

"Dan, you've got a big responsibility here, and I want to know that I can count on you. Nobody but you is accountable to see that your team is down there doing their job. We've got a reputation in Ramoco to keep our refinery tops in production."

"I'll do my best. By the way, Harry," he said, turning to face his boss. "I've got a guy on my shift who has some kind of a problem. I think he's drinking on the job. What should I do?"

"We've got a standard treatment for guys with substance abuse problems. Have him see Kathy in the first aid room, and sign him up."

"Well," Dan hesitated, "I don't think he's up to going public with his problem."

"It isn't my job—or yours—to deal with his tender feelings. Look, if he doesn't face up, tell him to use his willpower. Tell him to try harder. Remind him we've got objectives here that we've got to achieve before year's end. I don't want to hear any more about it, understand? I haven't got time for people like that."

"Harry," said the Woman, "two months later, Dan Harwood checked himself into an outpatient program for alcoholism."

"That's true about Dan, but what does listening have to do with it?"

"Didn't you realize that Dan was trying to tell you some of the emotional problems he himself was having? You left the refinery that night without ever knowing what was deeply troubling him, even though he was testing the waters and working up the courage to talk to you about it. He was trying to reach out for help," she explained. "He was sending out distress signals."

"Are you saying I was supposed to be able to figure all this out during that one meeting?" he asked skeptically. "I'm certainly not a mind reader or a psychiatrist."

"Good listening habits allow people to tell you what's on their minds so you don't have to wonder or second guess. It's not hard to do but it does require practice. And that's my job, Harry, to see that you get enough practice using this principle about listening and understanding."

"You really think listening makes such a big difference?"

"It surely does, Harry. Besides, learning to listen and understand are a part of your discretionary agreement. It's not an option."

———————◆◆◆———————

About a week later, Harry was back doing a full shift. As the refinery whistle announced the beginning of the morning shift, he called up the Monthly Operations Reports on his computer screen. He frowned at what he saw. The numbers fell short of his expectations and of his budget projections to headquarters. To improve during the next quarter, some drastic steps would have to be taken. The idea that came immediately to mind was cost-cutting.

Harry had a few major fixations in life, and cost-cutting was one of them. "Cut Costs" was another one of the mottos for living, like "Win at Any Cost," that he had inherited from his father.

"The Depression was the best business schooling I ever had," his father often used to say during reflective moments after dinner, while he was puffing on a Havana Cigar and drinking coffee. John Hartwell was one of those who survived the Depression without losing his pants. He always said that cost-cutting was what kept his pants on.

Even though Harry wasn't permitted to smoke cigars or drink coffee since his heart seizure, he wasn't required to give up his cost-cutting principles.

———◆◆◆———

The moment he decided that cost cutting would be the new motto for Ramoco happened to be the moment when Wesley Washington, head of maintenance at Ramoco, knocked on his office door.

Wesley was one of the few men at the refinery physically bigger and stronger than Harry, yet he was a man who was all heart. Harry used to say that Wes Washington was sweet as sugar.

"Hey, Harry!" Wesley grinned open-armed as he strode across the room to shake Harry's hand. "Glad to see you back, man. For a sailor recently out of sick bay, you aren't looking too bad."

During their time in the service, while Harry had paid his dues as a naval officer, Wes climbed the Army ranks to staff sergeant. He was proud of his military stint and fond of recalling it. Huge and lovable, Wes was as faithful and patriotic as they come, and he reflected the gentle disposition of a caring St. Bernard.

Harry did not know how to listen to St. Bernards. As far as he was concerned, they spent too much time wagging their tails, slurping, lapping, and hanging around without saying much. They never seemed to get down to business, and they annoyed him especially when the pressure was on, as it was now.

"I'm busy, Wes." Harry's voice was soft but curt. "What's on your mind?"

The genial man was thrown off balance by Harry's refusal to savor his "Welcome Home" and being categorized as bothersome at his first visit on his manager's return. Harry didn't even allow Wes the normal warm-up time warranted by the seriousness of his request.

"I was planning to talk to you about some needs we have in maintenance," replied Wesley.

"Uh-oh, here we go again," said Harry.

Wes was hurt by the comment but said nothing.

"I suppose," continued Harry, annoyed, "you want to bust through the ceiling and hire more maintenance people?"

"Well, I do," admitted Wes. He sensed the swing of Harry's executioner's axe in the air, but he had begun preparing for this meeting over a week ago, so he put his head right on the chopping block. "I would like you to authorize two more maintenance positions."

"Wes," said Harry with a patronizing chuckle, "we're trying to keep costs down here in the refinery. You know that as well as I do. Besides, we've got a reputation among all the U.S. Ramoco refineries of being the best cost-cutters."

Harry was sure his dad would be proud of him at this moment.

"I think if you study the problem closely, Wes, really concentrate on it, you'll see that it's really a management problem on *your* part."

Wes knew what the next step would be. It had happened a dozen times before. He would now be expected to listen politely to his own eulogy.

"I'm proud to have you on my team, Wes. You're a damn good maintenance supervisor. I know I can count on you to be a good cost-cutter."

"How predictable this guy is," thought Wesley.

But there was more.

"You're too nice a guy, Wes, too nice to those slippery pigs in maintenance who probably do little more than grunt as they go through the motions of working. Stick a prod in their behinds, and when they slack off, give them a jab or two. Let 'em bleed a bit. It won't hurt them."

Wesley winced again. He was angry now, as well as hurt. He didn't like anyone criticizing his maintenance people. As a team, they were hard-working—but overwhelmed by the sheer volume of breakdowns and repairs.

"Wes," Harry continued, "if you really think efficiency, I think you can get better mileage out of your crew." He came forward from behind his desk and was maneuvering Wes, past the Progress Chart Ann Laney had put up on his wall, toward the door.

"Now, for a few final words of blessing over my grave," thought Wesley cynically.

"You're a good manager, Wes," said Harry in his best coach-of-the-losing-team-at-half-time voice. "In tougher situations than this, you've pulled us out of rough spots and made it over the goal line. I know you can do it again, good buddy. Keep up the terrific work."

As Harry gave Wes a final shove out the door, he added, "Give me a written report in a few weeks just to prove to me that you've licked the problem. I'll bet you'll do it all in a short time."

As Harry closed the door, he smiled to himself, "Well, I sure handled that crisis."

Outside the door, a dejected Wesley Washington was muttering angrily to himself, "Okay, Harry, I guess I was wrong to believe that change-of-heart story some guys were telling about you. You haven't changed at all. You're the same old Harry, The Abominable NO Man."

Wes was so discouraged that he took off the rest of the day as personal leave time.

At lunch that day, Harry met Fred Schmidt, his engineering supervisor, in the cafeteria line.

"How's everything going, Fred?" asked Harry casually, as he picked up a salad to examine its contents.

"Okay, I guess. Actually, I'm concerned about equipment downtime."

"Equipment downtime," echoed Harry, absentmindedly. His eyes were looking at a grilled cheese sandwich he wasn't allowed to have.

"I think we have a serious problem with maintenance," Fred continued. "Equipment is falling apart repeatedly."

"Yeah, I know," Harry nodded. "Wes was in to see me this morning."

"Harry, there's no way we can meet this month's quota. I think we're drowning."

Harry missed the warning, because he was too busy listening to his own inner dialogue about cost-cutting, he already had a plate full of problems, and at the moment he was more interested in lunch.

"I'll see what I can do," said Harry, reaching for a cottage cheese and raw vegetable plate. "By the way, Fred, how's the family?"

Fred's "Fine" came as they parted near the desserts.

As Harry carried his cafeteria tray over to a table, the message hit him. "Oh, my God," he said to himself. "Wes was trying to tell me something and I didn't hear it. I think I blew it with Wes."

"I think you did, too," came the familiar Woman's voice inside his head. "Wes was throwing you a life preserver to save your sinking refinery and you didn't take it. You didn't listen and try to understand him. You threw him overboard and then gave him a pep talk, telling him he could save himself."

"Well, that's easy to fix," he said dismissing the problem. "I'll authorize the two maintenance people he wants."

Harry picked up his fork and was about to spear a piece of lettuce.

"I'm not here to control your business decisions, Harry, only your discretionary time," said the Woman. "I'm not concerned about hiring two new maintenance employees, but about the relationship with Wes that you violated by neither hearing nor understanding him."

"What's the rush? It's only noon. I've got twenty hours to replay the scene with Wes. I'll go see him right after lunch, if that's what you want," he replied, as he turned his attention back to the salad.

"No you won't, Harry. Wes was so dejected after talking to you this morning that he took off the rest of the day, figuring he'd be no good to anyone, in such a foul mood."

"So, I'll send for him as soon as I get in tomorrow morning," he said, wishing the Woman would go away and let him eat.

"If I remember your schedule correctly," she commented, "you're due over at headquarters across town for a big meeting first thing in the morning."

"Damn, that's right!" acknowledged Harry. "Can I have till tomorrow afternoon to fix it with Wes?" he asked her eagerly.

"No, Harry," said the Woman. "Your discretionary time runs out at, let me see, 8:35 tomorrow morning."

"Well, I guess I'm going to have to make a home visit."

"Now, you can eat your lunch," she said, pleased with his decision, "and I won't bother you."

Harry pulled up in front of 517 Fieldstone Road, got out of his steel grey Chrysler New Yorker, walked up to the front door, and rang the bell. He had never done a thing like this before: Going to an employee's home to apologize, to listen, and to make things right.

Wesley Washington was near forty years old, his wife was a social worker. With two teenaged children they lived in this middle class neighborhood along with a lot of other professional families their age. Hardly anyone came unexpectedly after supper, except friends of their children.

"Mr. Hartwell!" exclaimed a surprised Mrs. Washington, opening the front door. "Come in."

"Hi, Lorraine. Pardon the intrusion."

An equally startled Wesley Washington overheard the greeting at the front door, and hurried toward his guest.

"Harry, come on in. This is surely an unexpected honor."

"We need to talk, Wes."

"Sure, Harry. Right in here." He led the way into his study, and shut the door. "What's up?"

It had been difficult enough for Harry to come here. He didn't like to play "away" games. He preferred his own turf, his home field. But, here he was, and there was nothing to do but plunge forward.

"I didn't feel good about our conversation this morning, Wes."

That was the best Harry could do for an apology.

Wes was grateful for the gesture.

"When you requested the extra help in maintenance, I knew *what* it was you wanted, but I didn't take the time to hear the *why*."

Wesley could hardly believe that this was the unerring Harry Hartwell, standing before him like a reformed Scrooge on Christmas morning.

"By the way," Harry continued, "I'm sorry to intrude into your home at this hour, but it's important to me to find out what the score is in maintenance."

Wes was still incredulous. He could not hear Harry's discretionary clock ticking.

"Well, Harry," he began slowly, "I had been warming up to come see you for a long time. The problem is not a new one. But, man, it took me all these weeks to get up the courage to face you."

"I guess I've got a reputation for being hard-nosed about things like new expenses."

Harry was replaying in his own words what Wes had just said.

"You do put up a pretty scary front, Harry," agreed Wesley.

Sensing Harry was really listening, Wesley felt encouraged to go on.

"Downtime on machines has been increasing faster than I'd like. I've been obliged to call for a lot of overtime. The machinery breakdown problem is getting out of hand. My men are running from machine to machine, no time to do anything but first aid. But band-aids don't heal the problems we've got. Many of those turbines, compressors, and other rotating machinery need complete overhauls, but I don't have the manpower to do it. My people are burning out."

"Go on," encouraged Harry. "I'm listening. You're saying that the major weakness here is a bunch of machines that need a complete going-over, and all that your men have time for is a lick and a polish. And if we don't do something soon, the whole system will collapse."

"That's exactly right," said Wes nodding vigorously. "I support your cost-cutting efforts, man, but in my view two more maintenance people would lower machine downtime as well as my overtime costs."

"So, you're saying that we'll have to push up personnel costs in order to keep the refinery going?" Harry asked.

"No, Harry," said Wes, correcting Harry's misunderstanding. "Personnel costs will be more than offset by better efficiency, because the overhauled equipment will stay up and running for weeks on end."

"Let me see if I've got this straight," said Harry, reflecting what he had just heard. "You think, if we invest in two more people, our total costs will look better."

"Now, you've got my thinking." Wes was smiling.

"Why didn't you say this in the first place, this morning?" Harry asked.

"I wanted to. I had planned to. I even tried to, man, but you wouldn't listen. You threw me out of court before I could tell my side of things."

"I see that now," Harry admitted, putting his hand on the taller man's shoulder. "I was so fixated on cost-cutting this morning that I didn't give you a chance to present your case."

"I checked my ideas with engineering, too, and they support me one hundred percent."

"I know," added Harry. "I saw Fred in the cafeteria line at lunch today."

"I'm glad that made the difference," said Wesley. "I really want our refinery to be tops, and I know that we can do it."

Wesley gave him the thumbs-up sign with both hands.

"You go get the personnel you need first thing tomorrow," said Harry as he got up to leave. "I'm scheduled for a big huddle at headquarters in the morning, and I'll tell them what you said—that we'd be tops."

In his car driving home, Harry talked aloud to the Woman about his conversation with Wesley Washington.

"I'd say you get A+ in 'Hearing and Understanding' tonight, Harry," came the Woman's voice.

Even though he couldn't see her, he was sure she was smiling, proud of his performance.

"I'm a little pigheaded at times," he admitted, "but I do eventually learn my lessons. And tonight I learned the value of doing Listening Checks."

"Wes appreciated it when you gave him feedback to show that you were listening."

"And the times I missed his point, he set me straight because I gave him the space to do so."

"By restating what you thought he was saying," she said, "you allowed any misunderstandings to be cleared up immediately, not after long hours of working on the wrong problem or moving in the wrong direction."

"It's funny how we take communication skills for granted in business," Harry added, as he stopped his car at a red light. "I know there are lots of workshops on how to listen and how to communicate, but I never saw the value of them. I figured, 'Everyone is born with a mind and a mouth. What more does anyone need in order to communicate?'"

"You are discovering that listening is a skill that can be taught, learned, and developed," chimed in the Woman.

"It was difficult for me to admit that I was not a big-league listener," he explained, "especially since I prided myself on being so sharp. What an embarrassing discovery to find out, not only was I totally untrained in listening skills but I was not even giving people a chance to make their point. The fact is I just wasn't listening to guys like Wes."

"Actually, Harry, the only person you've been hearing up till now has been yourself. You've never had to deal with an opposing view, because as far as you were concerned an opposing view didn't exist."

"If I want to have a smoothly running team, I guess listening is one important tool for me to have."

"And Listening Checks are the key to communication success," added the Woman. "They are especially important when the outcome of the communication is crucial, as it was with Wesley."

"You're right." Then he took the idea one step further. "I'll bet summarizing the other person's words in Listening Checks would be really valuable on the telephone, when you can't see the other person's face or watch their reactions."

"That's a nice insight."

Harry put the turn signal on, and eased his car into his own driveway.

"You've really mastered the main points of hearing with understanding, Harry," commented the Woman. "Perhaps, when you get to have a job like mine, with discretionary clients, you can be put in charge of those with communication problems."

"No, thanks," said Harry, politely, as he shut off the ignition.

They both laughed at the image of Harry as a discretionary angel.

He had no desire to play her position on the Big Team. "I'm having enough trouble learning the basics just to save my life."

"Actually," corrected the Woman, "it's primarily your heart that you're saving."

Harry stepped out of the car and spoke in a whisper. "My understanding of what you just said is that your goal is to help put my heart back into my life. Is that true?" he asked in a Listening Check.

They both laughed again.

"By the way, I've been dying to ask you a question. Wait. Let me rephrase that. I've been very curious about something."

"Yes, Harry?"

"Do you have a name? I mean, I don't know what to call you."

"Sometimes I'm called Selena."

"I've never known anyone with that name."

"Now, you do."

"You know, I've never told Molly about you or about my discretionary deal. Frankly, I don't know how to talk about you. What do I say? How do I explain you? Won't people think I'm crazy?"

"I'm going to let you figure that one out, Harry," she replied, after a pause. "But, however you do it, do it with a sense of humor."

"You know, I think I'm finally getting to the point where I want to learn your principles for their own sake, not just to save my skin."

"Harry, thank you for that affirmation. I was beginning to wonder if you would ever say it."

He walked into his house with a smile on his face.

"*T*ell Me The Truth With Compassion"

Although Harry truly enjoyed being the general manager of the Ramoco refinery here in town, he had been dreaming for the past few years of being promoted to Vice President of U.S. Operations. He wanted to manage Ramoco Oil all over the United States. That's where the real power was.

Recently, he had been reviving that fantasy, but wondered if his mild heart seizure would penalize him and hurt his chances for a shot at a national position. In his mind, he argued that he had returned to work so quickly that his time away was not much more than a long holiday.

Today at lunch, Joel Silverman, Ramoco's corporate General Counsel, who had been with the company a dozen years, assured Harry that his heart trouble might be a minor negative factor but would ultimately not be fatal to his chances for the highly-coveted V.P. of U.S. Operations position.

Joel's reassurance was very welcome.

"Maybe I can actually pull it off," Harry thought.

Besides, as his Progress Chart revealed to anyone who cared to look at his office wall, he was shucking off weight at a steady pace. The doctor was proud of him, Molly was proud of him, and his executive assistant Ann Laney had been consistently pasting gold stars on his Chart, the kind her second-grade boy got for doing something noteworthy at school. He enjoyed looking at those gold stars on his Progress Chart as much as any eight-year-old.

When he returned from lunch with Joel Silverman, he found a memo on his desk. Hitting a tender spot in Harry's solar plexus, the message totally reversed his mood. He came storming from his office, fuming mad.

"Do you know what the Supreme Beanbag, Carl Harris, has done now?" he seethed.

Ann Laney was the only one around at the moment. "I'll bet it has something to do with that Memo to All Refinery Managers I left on your desk during lunch," replied Ann, cautiously, looking up from her word processor.

Harry stomped up to Ann's desk, shaking the memo in his hand, as if he hoped to shake the words themselves off the paper.

"That financial gestapo at headquarters has autocratically shelved the proposal I supported about instituting cafeteria-style fringe benefits for all Ramoco employees."

"You mean the one which would let each of us choose how much coverage we wanted for each benefit such as life insurance, pension plan, health benefits, day care, vacation, and so on?"

He nodded. "Neil Curtis, our top human resources guy, made the proposal at the last big headquarters meeting. I supported it because it gave our employees a lot of options and choices. And best of all, it would cost Ramoco not a dollar more than the old, rigid same-for-everybody plan we now have. It would have been one way to help everyone at Ramoco. And that idiot, Carl Harris, kiboshed it."

"It sounded like a great idea to me," said Ann. "Why would Mr. Harris be opposed to it?"

"Probably because he's got about as much originality as a cancelled stamp. The other day, I told Fred Schmidt that Harris only wants to flaunt his power around the country by using these annoyance tactics. He has the ear of the President and is able to squash any new strategy that comes down the pike, and he usually does just that whenever it is something he himself didn't propose. That guy is really out of date, a relic of the past, nothing but a useless souvenir, no more valuable than yesterday's boarding passes."

"Mr. Hartwell, the word going around the refinery is that Mr. Harris has his sights on the big job opening up in Ramoco next year, the same position you want."

Ann's comment only served to intensify the stinging emotion in Harry's gut. Even though Carl had just scored points with his memo, Harry was not giving up the struggle with his arch rival. The game was far from over. Harry would put some real pressure on him.

He edged forward to within inches of Ann's face.

"Anyone who goes up against Harry Hartwell," he hissed, "lives to regret it."

"I'm sure he'll be sorry he wanted that job, Mr. Hartwell," whispered Ann, shifting nervously. She found it uncomfortable to be near him when he was in a mood like this.

"When I get done with that huckster, the only job in the world left for him will be to sell peanuts and popcorn in the bleachers," he said as he backed into his office.

Ann Laney knew enough to be silent. In her imagination she could picture Harry's angry exhaust fumes aimed toward Carl Harris, sending him into a fit of coughing and choking.

———— ◆•◆ ————

During a phone call that came from Joel just then about some oil rights, Harry took the time with the company's top lawyer to spit out some more of his anger at Carl.

"He is nothing but a mindless calculator," Harry began.

"Sounds like a typical day at Ramoco, USA," said Joel, who was well aware of the rivalry between Carl and Harry.

"He may claim to be a financial wizard at headquarters," Harry continued, "but he knows diddly squat about the oil business."

"I'll bet our next board meeting will be a hot one," commented Joel.

"When it comes to big league oil politics, refining, and field drilling operations, he's nothing but a smudge."

"Harry, have you considered washing your face in cold water?"

Harry didn't even hear the lawyer's teasing. "No oil smarts in his brain, only ooze. Besides, he's got all the worst qualities of a calculator—rigid, inflexible, colorless."

"Cool down, Harry. I know where you're coming from. Carl sat on your idea, and that's hard to take, for anybody."

"It wasn't even mine, it was Neil's. He couldn't appreciate a new idea like this one if it bit him through the seat of his pants. In fact, if you take Harris away from his computer, you've taken off his pants."

"Look, Harry," said Joel softly, "I know it's good to get your anger off in a safe place, and I'm glad you've dumped it now. But you've got to keep going forward."

"That guy's always putting up road blocks and detours."

"Don't use up all your gas getting angry at Carl." Joel's voice was soothing. "It's not worth it."

———————◆◗●◖◆———————

After hanging up the phone, Harry began pacing back and forth in his office. While his imagination was inventing ways to get back at Carl, he heard the familiar voice inside his head.

"Sounds like you're really angry at Carl Harris."

"You bet I am," agreed Harry vehemently. "People like Neil Curtis sweat for months to come up with innovative plans for Ramoco like this one, and Harris just rubs them out with his heel. As far as he's concerned, people's good ideas are no more than cigarette butts."

"I think it's about time we tackled Principle Three, Harry," she began tactfully. "Do you remember it?"

"It's hard to think nice thoughts when that slime is on my mind."

"He's the reason I brought up Principle Three," the Woman said, "because the discretionary clock has been ticking away, at least since your phone call with Joel."

"So, how did I mess up Principle Three?" he asked as he glanced down. He had all five principles written out, for ready reference. "Principle Three says: *Tell Me the Truth With Compassion*," recited Harry. "I didn't violate that principle," Harry assured her. "I certainly told Joel the truth about Carl Harris. Or, am I missing something?"

"The principle is about constructive confrontation," the Woman said.

"Constructive confrontation sounds more like a new offensive strategy for a football team than a principle for managing from the heart."

"There are times when you need to confront people, Harry," she continued, "like your need to confront Carl. This principle tells you not to avoid the confrontation, but to do it with firmness and caring."

For Harry, caring for Carl would be about as easy as swallowing a dead rat. However, he could hear the discretionary clock ticking.

"Do you plan to give Carl the benefit of your reactions to his memo?" she asked.

"No. It wouldn't do any good. Trying to change Carl's mind is like trying to beat Superman in arm wrestling."

"Harry, I sense a small problem."

"What's that?" he asked, squirming.

"It appears that you do not intend to tell Carl the truth about your response to his memo—with or without compassion."

"This principle shouldn't apply in totally futile situations," said Harry vehemently.

"Where you think this principle should or should not apply doesn't matter. It applies universally, and it applies here."

"What are you saying?"

"I'm saying that the discretionary clock is ticking over your response to Carl's memo."

"Aw, come on! Give me a break!" Harry pleaded. "I've done pretty well on the other principles."

"Harry, you are not reading a menu, where you can pick and choose which principles you like or when you will or will not adhere to them," insisted the Woman. "According to our agreement, all of the five principles for managing from the heart apply all of the time. There are no exceptions. Not even Carl Harris."

"Well, it's not going to do any good in his case."

"The effect your confrontation has on Carl's behavior is up to Carl. Your responsibility is to tell him the truth with compassion concerning what you think about his memo."

Her message was painfully clear to Harry. "Sometimes I think I signed a bad contract with you." For the life of him, Harry could not see any constructive purpose to be served by leveling with Carl.

"Any time you decide you want to cancel," said the Woman, "the choice is yours."

Harry weighed the options for only a few seconds before he decided.

"I'll call him."

"Good," she replied.

"So, how do I do it? What's the game plan?"

"The first step is to speak directly to the person you need to confront, rather than to talk about him to others. You have been talking a lot to others about Carl Harris and his memo, but not saying a word to Carl."

"You mean this principle won't even allow me to cut him to ribbons behind his back?"

"Correct," answered the Woman.

Harry wanted to make sure how much liberty he could take without actually violating the principle. Now he knew.

"The next step is to address Carl in a way that's respectful. Even though he may have made a mistake or even been harmful to others, you must confront him in a way that allows him to keep his dignity."

"You want me not only to talk directly to Carl but to do it respectfully and make him feel dignified, and all the while he's got a poisoned dart aimed at me?" It was incredulous to Harry that anyone who knew him would even think of asking him to speak to Carl that way. He felt outraged.

The Woman waited patiently.

Harry was trying to think of a way to avoid the confrontation with Carl yet not renege on his agreement with the Woman.

"In theory," he began, "it's a great idea to treat people with respect. Actually, it sounds a bit like Principles One and Two again, I mean, not making the other person wrong and listening to what they say and how they understand things."

"Yes," agreed the Woman patiently.

"So, I've got to tell Carl Harris the truth with compassion, is that it?"

"That's it. No way around it."

Harry knew when he had lost the fight.

"Okay, here goes." He picked up the phone and punched out Carl's number. Nothing in the rules said he couldn't take out his anger punching the keys.

"Hello, is Carl there? . . . Hi, Carl. Harry here. . . . Yes, I'm feeling fine. . . . Thanks. . . . Listen, Carl, I'm really calling about your memo on cafeteria fringe benefits."

"I suspected as much, Harry. I knew some people would be disappointed about the delay, but we just don't know enough about the long-term financial implications of the proposal to dive into it."

"It didn't seem to me that we were *diving* into it." He emphasized the word but was careful to keep anger out of his voice. "In fact, Neil Curtis did months of research on the idea before he proposed it."

"I'm sure he did," added Carl noncommittally.

"Anyway," continued Harry, "what I wanted to say was that I think you dumped a great opportunity. It was a chance for Ramoco to gain a leg up for our folks, and with your decision I think Ramoco has blown that chance."

"Thanks for letting me know your opinion, Harry."

Harry couldn't tell whether Carl was really hearing his opinion, or just doing a "thank you for sharing" routine as a polite dismissal.

"I don't think we blew it at all, Harry," Carl continued. "The plan hasn't been rejected, only delayed. You'll have a chance to be involved in studying, reviewing, and revising the plan over the next year, so that when and if we do implement it, it will be the best plan for all concerned, the employees as well as the corporation."

Harry gripped the phone harder and gritted his teeth as Carl's emotionless, rational voice poured into his ear. His only hope was to get off the phone. "I just wanted you to know how I felt."

"I welcome your input," said Carl.

"Okay," said Harry as he hung up the phone.

"There!" Harry said to the Woman, relieved that it was over. "Was that compassionate enough for you?"

"You certainly took a minimalist approach to Principle Three," said the Woman. "Your confrontation passes muster, Harry, but barely."

"With Carl, I couldn't get off the phone quickly enough."

"Why get off the phone?"

"I don't think you understand the stakes riding on this," explained Harry. "When the current Vice President of U.S. Operations retires next year, Carl is angling for that job."

"What's the matter with that?"

"What's the matter with it is that I'm looking forward to getting that job myself. And I don't want that clod to ace me out. Aside from being a nerd, he's in my way."

"Does Carl have any positive traits at all, as far as you are concerned?" she asked.

"Hell, yes! He's smart. Smart as they come. A regular fox. He's a first-rate CFO," his voice dropped to a whisper, "but only third-rate when it comes to oil politics. The OPEC snipers would cripple him with their first round of shots."

"And it seems unfair to you that your obligation to manage people from the heart should apply even to your chief rival for promotion?"

"Damn right!" There was not a shadow of doubt in Harry's mind about that answer.

"Sometimes," said the Woman, "life is unfair, Harry."

A few days later, Harry was pacing around his office nervously jangling the coins in his pocket and repeatedly looking at his watch. In ten minutes, Wesley Washington was scheduled to knock on his door to receive his Annual Performance Review.

"Are you ready for Wesley?" asked the Woman's voice inside his head.

"Not really," admitted Harry. "One thing that bugs me about Wes is that he gives poor performers on his team a free ride. With hard workers, Wes is a great boss. But with those who screw up on the job, he is entirely too tolerant. A maintenance man would have to set off a bomb in the refinery before Wes would say anything to him. He hates to be anything but Mr. Nice Guy. I wish there was some way I could get him to confront his troublesome people earlier on, to lower his threshold of confrontation. Then he could talk to people about their problems and not have to come asking me for more staff."

"It seems to me you have all the necessary ingredients of a great performance review for Wes."

"I haven't actually decided to tell him all this confrontation stuff. I don't know how he'll react."

"That's right," agreed the Woman. "Telling the truth with compassion means you lay out all the truth, and you can't predict anyone's reactions. But prediction is not your job when you manage from the heart. Your job is to acknowledge to Wes all the good qualities and behaviors you observed in him—you should be very clear in spelling them out first. Then, you tell him the truth in a helpful way about the areas where you think he's not doing a good job. In this case, you don't think he's very good about confronting poor performers. Right?"

"Right," agreed Harry. "But if I tell him the truth, don't I end up making him wrong?"

"First, you affirm him," explained the Woman. "Once he knows that you value him, he will probably want to improve his performance just as much as you want him to."

"I guess that makes sense," he acknowledged, still a bit confused.

"Otherwise," she continued, "where or when would Wesley ever get the benefit of your perceptions about him? When would he ever get to see the troublesome issues from your point of view? And how would he ever get a chance to improve his performance?"

"It's probably too much to expect these skills were issued to him with his genes." He shrugged. "I guess I could talk to him about it."

"That's a good idea. Wesley is a relatively young man, and this is his first management job, other than being a line foreman. Unless you're willing to show him and teach him, when is he ever going to learn the skills he needs to be a good manager?"

"You're right," he admitted. "But, according to you, I'm probably not the best-equipped person to do it. I'm not good with coach's jargon."

"That's probably true, but it does happen to be your job right now, and you *can* do it."

"So, how do I go about it?"

"You could work backwards," she began. "Look at the result you both want, namely, to help poor performers improve their performance. Figure out with him what he needs to do to get that result and how you can help him get it. You, too, can be part of the solution."

"That seems like a good place to start. I'll give it a try."

"Don't talk just about the problem. Remember to start by reviewing all his good traits. That's the primary and most important part of a performance review."

"Why should I tell him all that stuff?" asked Harry, genuinely puzzled. "Everybody knows that Wes is a great guy," he added. "It's not news."

"He'd love to hear it anyway," coached the Woman. "Let's rehearse some of the nice things you could say to Wesley."

Harry swallowed hard and squirmed in his chair. Harry's father had never told him anything about this affirmation stuff. Like classroom teachers of an earlier era, John Hartwell had always emphasized what his son did wrong. On tests in school, only Harry's wrong answers were marked in red. Similarly at home, his father never paid any attention to what he did correctly. Affirmations were not common when Harry was growing up. With his employees, Harry carried on the family tradition of focusing only on what was inadequate or unacceptable.

"Everybody loves Wesley. I like him, too," Harry admitted. "He does wonders with our mechanical equipment. This place is not what I would call our newest or most technically up-to-date refinery. Sometimes I think the equipment here comes from an ancient civilization. And Wes keeps it operational. That's a miracle in itself. In addition, he is one dedicated employee. Our most valuable player. I don't know what I would do without him. He maintains a five-star relationship with everyone. Except for the few goldbrickers on maintenance, the rest of his team of refinery troubleshooters worship the ground he walks on and would sell their mothers to help him keep the refinery running up to capacity."

"That's the idea," encouraged the Woman. "That's exactly the way to start his Performance Review. Keep up the good words. Here comes Wesley now."

It was hard for Harry's usually sharp tongue to speak the new language of affirmations, but after a bit of hesitancy the words did begin to flow. By the time he was three minutes into the interview, Wesley Washington was convinced that Harry considered him a very dedicated and highly-valued employee.

As difficult as it was for Harry to say good things, it was even more so for him to take the next step: confronting with compassion. But he began anyway.

"Even though you are one of the most powerful forces in this refinery, Wes, you have one blind spot. I think you know it, but I'm going to mention it again. And I hope together we can do something about it. You are such a nice guy, Wes, that certain employees take advantage of you. Consequently, when you get poor performance from any of your people, you don't deal with it. You don't follow through. You're too easy on those who cut corners."

"I know that, Harry."

"I'm really not the best example of confronting for you to follow," admitted Harry, "because I haven't ever confronted you about this problem in a constructive way before. Oh, yes, I've bitched up a storm about you being too easy with slowpokes in maintenance, but I've never taken the next step, namely, showing you how to throw the ball properly."

"Go ahead, boss, I'm listening. I still have a thing or two to learn before I retire," said Wesley with a smile. "It was only when I was a teenager that I was sure I knew everything."

Wes' attempt at humor relaxed Harry a bit, and he leaned back in his chair. "Here goes, Wes."

For Harry, it was his second session on Principle Three—the phone call with Carl had been the first—but he found he was enjoying it more than he could have imagined.

"At the same time as you're asking me for more people in maintenance," he said to Wesley, "I want to ask you to tell the maintenance people who are copping out on the job to get in shape. I'm not talking about the tried and true employees, but the major rule-violators. I'm talking, for example, about that one guy who annually wins the world absentee record—you know who I mean?"

Wesley nodded in agreement. "You're right, Harry, that guy is a prize, but he's been a Ramoco employee for twenty-five years."

"You believe that, because an employee has been with us for twenty-five years, he deserves special treatment?"

"That's the way I've thought about it, so I don't belabor the fact that he's out a lot."

"In any case, we need to find out what's going on with him. I don't know whether the guy has a drinking problem, a girl friend on the side, is into drugs, or what. All I know is he is more like a visitor than an employee. And you have another guy who always rushes in twenty minutes late. He seems to have lost the ability of showing up on time."

Wesley nodded again. "I'll admit his maintenance team is usually always the last to get out into the refinery, but his team is probably the best we've got."

"So, you feel if his team is effective, you can tolerate a bit of tardiness."

"Harry, I can't afford to upset my best maintenance team."

"I see. And there's one other guy," Harry continued, "who has a destructive touch. Every piece of equipment he fixes collapses within the hour and ends up in worse shape than before. Maybe the guy needs some technical training, or retraining."

"He's another twenty-five year veteran. He's been wrecking things since before I came on board."

"And your policy is to leave old timers alone?"

Wesley's head continued nodding assent.

Harry took a deep breath and went on.

"Wesley, I don't have confidence that you're confronting these people, finding out what's going on, and taking the steps necessary to clean up their act. I consider you a top performer, a man I can really count on. But there are times when being non-demanding doesn't really help your work or the company. What I want to know is, first, are you willing to confront those buzzards and find out what is really going on? And, second, how can I support you?"

"If I confront these guys," said Wesley hesitantly, "I'm afraid the situation will get worse."

"From your always-the-nice-guy point of view I can see your fear, Wes, but think about it for a minute. Nothing could be worse than the present situation. You yourself told me the bottom was falling out."

Wesley reluctantly agreed. "Look, Harry," he said, "my men are not perfect, but if I were to lose the ones I've got, I could get somebody worse, someone who couldn't fill their shoes."

Harry realized that this might be an opportune moment to practice Principle Two and listen for understanding.

"So, Wes, your fear is that if you take steps to confront the poor performers, they'll just quit, and their replacements might be even worse."

Wes sighed heartily. "Exactly."

Having listened with understanding and having received a sign of agreement from Wesley, he was ready to do some truth-telling. "It might not really hurt to get some of those flatfoots out of your army. We've got battles to win, and these guys, if they stay the way they are, will only continue to slow everything down, and we'll all lose."

Wesley realized that his defense was just so much smoke, and that Harry was right.

Harry sensed it, too. "Wes, I can tell you that your all-around performance is championship level and your contribution to the success of this refinery is immense. There's no danger that you will ever lose your job here, even if you don't agree to confront those guys."

"I know I should do it," acknowledged Wesley. "It's only that I'd like to squirm out of it. It's not in my nature to stick a gun in anyone's face."

"So, it's distasteful for you to be confrontational," Harry reflected.

"Right," replied Wesley. "You got it."

"But it certainly is in your nature to be a great superintendent, Wes. This is only one small area of improvement you could use. So, are you willing to try it, with my support? And, if so, I'd like an agreement between us that you will at least talk to each of those three problem guys I mentioned."

Harry realized that he really cared about Wesley Washington and wanted him to succeed. He felt it in his heart.

After a few moments of silence, Wesley Washington held out a sincere but anxious hand for Harry to shake.

"We can't let too much time pass before you lose your courage," Harry added as he put his hand on Wesley's shoulder, "so I want you to tell me by what deadline you will have confronted these people. At our next review meeting we will celebrate your victory. When should we meet?"

"How's two weeks sound, Harry?"

"Two weeks is fine with me. And if you need any support, you come see me, okay?"

They shook hands and smiled at each other.

———◆◗◉◖◆———

All in all, Harry felt he was succeeding. Molly had noticed an increased gentleness in her husband, and people at work were commenting on how much Harry had changed in the past weeks.

The Woman also seemed pleased with his progress.

They often had their coaching sessions as he did his two-mile walks in the mornings and evenings. Much as he might deny it, he enjoyed talking to her, even though the time together was unmistakably a training session.

He had been doing well practicing Principles One and Two. He was no longer making people *wrong* very often, and when he did he cleaned up his mess quickly.

He was also learning to hear and understand, as Principle Two recommended, though he found it difficult. But she had predicted that. For him, it was too easy to enter a meeting with his mind closed, or at least already made up. He told the Woman he thought she was considerate in letting him tackle the principles one by one.

"The principles build on one another," she explained. "Each new principle assumes the principles that went before it. Principle Three counts on what you've learned before."

"So, in general," Harry asked the Woman on one of his morning walks, "when do I need to do this constructive confrontation?" He had already racked up a couple of successes with Principle Three, or at least with parts of it, so this was a review session as far as he was concerned.

"When something isn't going the way it should and needs to be changed, that's when it's time to tell the truth with compassion."

"You mean, when the maintenance people are filling out work orders improperly, or truckers are delivering refined products to the wrong shipping dock, or a supervisor is spending money without proper authorization, or a foreman is giving workmen incorrect instructions or no instructions at all?

"Or when someone like Harry Hartwell isn't managing from the heart," the Woman added with a touch of gentleness. Harry had been a hard nut to crack, probably one of the hardest she ever had.

"So, if something goes wrong," he said, getting back on track, "I shouldn't make their heads roll. Otherwise, I can't keep relating to them."

"Most people who have to confront someone," the Woman added, "tend to do radical surgery, when only minor alterations are needed. The two most common extreme forms are either to fire the offender or to refuse ever again to communicate with him."

"I've done my share of those," he admitted. "But now it's time to polish up my technique. Give Principle Three to me in a nutshell."

"There are three steps to it. The *first step,* as I said before you phoned Carl Harris the other day, is to speak directly to the person you need to confront, rather than to talk about him or her to others. You had been talking a lot to others about Carl Harris and his memo, but not saying a word to Carl."

"Okay, I've got that one down. What's next?"

"The *second step* is to address the other person in a way that's respectful. Even though people may make a mistake or even harm others, you can confront them in a way that allows them to keep their dignity."

"I was able to do that with Carl, so I guess I can do it with anybody."

"The *third step* in practicing Principle Three is to see that the behavior needing correction gets changed."

"This is where you tell them what you want them to do, right?"

"Sort of," granted the Woman. "There are generally two cases. Case A is where the person is doing something hurtful or harmful, I mean, hurting you, harming someone else, or potentially destroying the whole organization. That kind of behavior must change quickly, and your job is to get that person to agree to change as soon as possible."

"Here's an example of Case A," offered Harry. "A few weeks ago, when the maintenance troubleshooters working with strong acids refused to wear safety gear, they could have gotten blinded or scarred their skin permanently, and they could have gotten the refinery fined for safety violations, and we'd lose our insurance. That kind of behavior has to change fast."

"Right," she said, and continued. "Case B is when the persons are doing a good job in general but improvement in behavior is needed. In a case like that, you offer to coach them and let them decide whether they want to change or not."

"I'm not sure I like the theory behind that second case," he decided. "As I understand it, if you leave the choice up to people whether or not they change, you're giving them the right of refusal."

"That's correct."

"We'd get nowhere if I followed that advice. Take Wes Washington in maintenance. You know as well as I do that he has lazy goons working for him and, when he let's them choose what they want to do, they get away with murder."

"It depends whether you're dealing with someone more like Wesley Washington or someone more like his poorly-performing employees," she clarified. "With Wes, remember, you gave him a choice. He wasn't in danger of losing his job whether he changed or not. But in other cases," the Woman added, "if people refuse to improve, there are consequences."

"I see," he acknowledged. "Like my discretionary clock."

"That's right. You give the other person a compassionate chance to change. If they refuse to, then you can take proper action. The point is, you never close the door to communication and change.

"All this sounds good in theory," he concluded in all honesty. "I'm not sure I believe every bit of it, especially when it comes to productivity, but I'm willing to do what I have to in order to keep that clock turned off."

"For your assurance, Harry, telling the truth with compassion can help increase productivity. Look at it this way. Unless you tell people the truth with compassion, it's impossible for them to know whether they are actually making a contribution in your eyes. Telling the truth with compassion not only helps people know where they stand in productivity or anything else, it also helps them understand, as you see it, their contribution to whatever it is they're working on. So, to get the best in productivity from people, they need to know the whole truth."

"Good and bad, right? Like me knowing the truth when I've set the discretionary clock running again."

"Harry, you have always taken pride in telling the truth, even if it sometimes hurts."

"Yes, I have," he replied confidently. "That's one of my top values."

"On the other hand, any strength used to an excess can become a liability."

"So, I shouldn't tell the truth sometimes?"

"I'm not suggesting you not tell the truth. What I am suggesting is that there are different ways to tell people the truth. For example, do you remember Ralph Weatherby?"

"Yes, I do. He had a lot of potential as an assistant refinery manager. Why he left us so suddenly has always puzzled me."

"Well, maybe I can shed some light on the situation. Ralph's performance as a young manager was very good, right?"

"Yes."

"He had high marks on productivity figures and product quality was excellent. His relationships with salaried and non-exempt personnel was good. Union grievances were down during his tenure. He was doing a good job in nearly every measure."

"That's correct."

"Ralph had risen through the ranks at Ramoco, the same way you did, from hourly worker to assistant refinery manager. And he was extremely loyal."

"That's why it didn't add up when he left us high and dry, and went to work for a competitor. That's not much gratitude in exchange for all we had done for him over the years, wouldn't you say?"

"So you don't know why he left?" the Woman asked.

"I don't have a clue," admitted Harry. "I was stunned by his betrayal."

"And you never asked him why he put the letter of resignation on your desk?"

"No."

"More importantly," said the Woman, changing the direction of the discussion, "I want you to consider how you confronted him on a performance issue. Maybe that will clarify the usefulness of Principle Three."

"Go ahead. I'm listening."

"It was a particularly hectic quarter, when orders were pouring in and Ralph's attention was focused on problems of production, quality, and maintaining his goal on turn-around time. Ralph allowed inventories to go dangerously low. When you received the regular inventory trend reports, you became extremely upset and chewed him out royally."

"Of course. I read him the riot act," he replied. "Running out of inventory is serious business. You can't play baseball unless you have balls and bats, and you can't sell refined oil products unless you have sufficient crude on hand."

"That's certainly right," she acknowledged. "And you were correct in being on top of the issue and confronting Ralph about it. In terms of Principle Three, that was step one. However, step two never occurred."

"What do you mean?"

"Your conversation with Ralph was entirely one way. You gave him no opportunity to respond to you. It is possible that he had a legitimate explanation. Furthermore, you could have given him credit for all the other things he was doing effectively."

"But none of those others things would have been worth beans without enough inventory. I can't give him credit unless he does the *whole* job, not just part of it."

"The point is that, when Ralph got no credit from you for all of the good things he had done, he was hurt and angry. He felt punished by you. After that encounter, he began looking for another job."

"So, you're saying I'm to blame for Ramoco losing Ralph? I drove him away?"

"No, we're not talking about anyone being blamed or at fault," she explained. "What I want you to remember is this different way of confronting. Ralph did not feel any appreciation from you. He did not sense that you valued him as a person. Or even as an employee. This could have been avoided if you had done step two, that is, listened to his side of the story and expressed appreciation for what he was doing well, and, step three, coached him on ways he could do a better job of inventory control."

"You talk as though Weatherby didn't do anything wrong. You talk about my driving Weatherby away from Ramoco. The truth is he drove Ramoco—all of us—up to within one inch of the cliff's edge!"

Harry was angry. He still resisted Principle Three. It seemed *unnatural* to him. It certainly seemed unnatural when he had to enhance Carl Harris' dignity! It now seemed unnatural to be told that he should have expressed gratitude to someone who almost plunged his refinery into financial disaster.

"You're telling me I ought to have been grateful to Weatherby? You've got the story a bit twisted. He ought to have been grateful to me."

"No, Harry," she calmly replied, "you have had years of experience in the oil business and could have been helpful to Ralph. And, with a little bit of caring, you would have ensured his loyalty to you and Ramoco. The thing to remember, Harry, is to confront with compassion. At home, when parents confront a child, they don't drive the child away. A good parent always lets a child know it is loved despite the problems of the moment."

"Look, home and work are two different places," he reasoned. "My job is not to be a big daddy to my subordinates."

"That is true, Harry. But keep in mind you are a powerful person in their eyes. What to you may seem a whisper, they may hear as a shout. Let's face it, the result you want is employees who are dedicated, motivated, and productive. And you can get that more effectively by showing more caring and compassion, especially when you confront them."

"I understand what you're saying," he admitted, "but it's hard for me. Besides, deep down, I'm afraid that if I play softie they might take advantage of me."

"That seems logical," she said, "but in reality just the opposite is usually true. When people feel you care about them and won't crush them, they are much more willing to listen to you and learn from you because they want to avoid mistakes and accomplish more."

"Remember To Look For My Loving Intentions"

With a smile on his face, Harry walked briskly in the evening air. It felt good to be alive.

After his physical examination this afternoon, grey-bearded Doctor Stuart had said, "Good, Harry. Everything looks very good. Keep on doing what you're doing."

And he had said, "Doc, all my life I've been a gamer. I'm not ready to go gently into the night."

The doctor gave Harry his standard pep talk at the end of every visit: "Eat healthy, Harry. No red meats. No butter. No alcohol. No caffeine. No nicotine. One aspirin every day. That's the magic formula. Plus plenty of exercise for your heart. You can heal yourself a lot better than I can. Remember that, because that's the reason you're paying me—to remind you about the fastest way to help you help yourself get better."

Harry liked that old codger, and trusted him. Dr. Preston Stuart was probably the only person on earth who could tell Harry to stop eating juicy sirloins, cut out cigars, and drink mint tea instead of a martini.

There was no denying that Doc's system was working. Harry's new diet would continue to keep him alive and in good health—as long as he also learned to manage from the heart.

***

"How are we doing?" Harry asked the Woman, as he turned off the sidewalk and onto a path through a wooded area.

He liked to think of his work with her in terms of a player and his coach. He couldn't do it without her, and, as far as he could tell, she wouldn't have a job if it weren't for him.

"It's about time for Principle Four," came her reply.

"'_Remember to Look for My Loving Intentions_,'" recited Harry confidently. "I was reviewing the list of principles on my desk this afternoon, trying to figure out what this one really meant."

"It's about listening," she replied, "like Principle Two. Only this one is on a deeper level."

"Principle Two is *'Hear and Understand Me,'* right?"

"Yes. That principle was about content, *what* people were saying. It asked you to listen carefully and clearly enough so you could reflect back in your own words what a person just said."

"I think I do that a lot now," he said.

"You do," she agreed, "but now you are ready to take that principle to a new level. You need to hear more than content alone. You need to listen for the *intention* behind what a person says."

"I'm always doing that," he replied confidently. "I couldn't survive in big business if I didn't do that. I have to watch carefully that suppliers don't cut corners on orders or try to sell me some crackpot idea. There are lots of sharp operators out there, and for some of them ethics isn't too high on their list of priorities."

"Harry," she interrupted, "Principle Four is not about looking out for crooked vendors. It requires that you turn your suspicious approach completely around. Up till now, you have been looking for people's *evil* intentions. This principle asks you to look for their *loving* intentions, something you don't do very much of."

"Why would I want to do that?" he asked honestly.

"Probably because in the long run it's going to help your production."

"What do you mean?"

"Not looking for a loving intention is a subtle way of looking for devious motives," she explained. "People sense where you're coming from. If you don't trust them, they probably won't feel they are worthy of making a contribution, so they won't bother to assume much responsibility and won't put in all the effort they would if you had looked for their loving intentions."

"You want me to trust everyone?"

"Not necessarily. Even when you don't trust someone, even when you don't like what they say or do, the idea of this principle is to look behind their words and actions for their positive intentions."

"Whoa! Wait a minute!" Harry held up his hand as if he were stopping traffic. "Now you're saying 'positive intentions.' Before, it was 'loving intentions.' Which is it? What am I supposed to be looking for?"

"To me, they are two ways of saying the same thing. I know you're not comfortable with the word 'loving.'"

"That's right. 'Loving' is not in the business world's vocabulary."

"Not yet, but someday it will be. Business is part of life, it can't be walled off. When you want a positive result for other people and your wish comes from the heart, your intentions are loving as well as positive."

"If people always had loving intentions," he asked, "then why are there so many business people in jail? Remember that guy in Accounting who worked for Carl Harris, the one that embezzled $15,000. Where's the loving intention in that?"

"I don't condone embezzlement, Harry, but it so happens that the man had mounting hospital bills for his wife's terminal illness."

"I'm sorry about that. I can see that a person like you might presume he was using the take to pay the doctor, but he might just as well have lost it gambling or spent it getting high. How can I possibly manage an oil refinery if I spend all my time hunting around for nonexistent loving intentions?" He decided to take an offensive approach with the Woman. Maybe I can have Principle Four crossed off the list, he thought.

"I'm managing a business," he said, "not running a weekend workshop for love birds. Haven't you ever heard of the business principles: Dog Eat Dog, or Every Man For Himself? Listen, in my business you never let a supplier take a lead farther than the length of a baseball bat. You know what happens to a pitcher, with a runner on base, who pitches without ever looking to see how big a lead the runner is taking?"

The Woman didn't reply, so he answered his own question.

"The runner steals second base. He'd be stupid not to, since that's the way the game is played. I mean, in business, especially the oil business, people take advantage of you as soon as you take your eyes off them. That's the last thing a pitcher wants, to have a runner in scoring position. When that runner scores, it means the opponents get ahead and you don't. A business succeeds only if the pitcher is vigilant. Why, if I hadn't noticed those inventory trend reports and caught the emergency situation, Ralph Weatherby would have cost our refinery a bundle."

"Harry, you must admit that in all he was doing Ralph had a loving intention."

"I guess he might have," Harry conceded. Then with a tug at his sleeve, he countered, "But a lot of good it did us."

He tried a new approach on the Woman.

"I don't know whether you have competitive business markets up there where you come from, but down here on the big league playing field it's 'Win or Lose' and 'Winner Take All.' The rule I live by is: 'Win! Win! Win!' In the end, winning is the only thing that counts. And loving only gets in the way."

She didn't buy it. He noticed a slight edge in her tone.

"Harry, what I am asking—no, requiring—you to do is to turn your suspicious attitude completely around. Your employees are capable of loving. They do not put on monster masks at the refinery door. When they punch in at the time clock, they do not turn into malevolent machines, they remain the same persons who kissed their kids or their spouse good-bye a little while before. Don't you think business would probably see a lot more loving behavior at work if people made it okay to have a heart from nine to five?"

"I follow your reasoning so far," he said in a conciliatory way. "And I sort of agree with your principle, but the loving part makes me nervous. Find a way for me to get into this principle a bit more smoothly. It's just not been my way of doing business."

"Okay," she said patiently. "Let's review this principle with Ramoco employees in mind." The encouragement in her tone reminded him that she was still his coach, and that if he did have an opponent, he had only to look in the mirror. At that moment, he was grateful that patience was a heavenly virtue.

He came to the end of the wooded area and was back on the sidewalk again approaching a block of small shops.

"I can see," the Woman conceded, "how you might not yet be ready to look for the loving intention in people from other companies. But in your own refinery, surely you can remember to look for positive intentions your employees may have for the success of Ramoco, can't you?"

Harry stopped dead in his tracks again.

"Are you kidding?" he yelled. "Everybody in my refinery having loving intentions? That's a great joke." He guffawed. "For one example," he continued, "Wes Washington's three good-for-nothing maintenance men aren't even in the ball park of loving intention. They care squat for Ramoco."

"This principle doesn't say you must *find* loving intentions everywhere," she explained, "but to *look* for them. They may not be present in certain situations, but your challenge is to remember to look for them, not just to presume they don't exist."

"I know enough not to waste my energy on certain duds in this refinery. I know who my friends are and who my enemies are."

"Harry, would you say at this moment that you are basically committed to not-trusting?" asked the Woman.

"I'm saying the business world is about not-trusting. And your principle of loving intentions simply can't apply across the board. It doesn't always work. For instance, if I were a jewelry shop owner and I saw some creepy-looking guys standing outside my display window, I think I'd lock my door. I wouldn't assume those thugs were possible customers. I would assume they were thugs and wanted to rob me. So, I take precautions. I want to protect my life and my property. What's wrong with that?"

"There's nothing wrong with taking precautions, Harry, but you talk as though you have closed off the possibility that certain people have loving intentions."

"What kind of loving intentions can thugs and lazy people have?"

"I agree there is a point where the intentions of such people may be so perverse and over-rationalized that it is unsafe to trust, but certainly at your refinery you can take a minute or two to look for loving intentions and come up with something."

"I still submit Wes' goldbrickers as Exhibit Number One."

"You're not always going to find a loving intention, Harry. There is evil in the world. There are people who do unspeakable things. The point of this principle is to look, and in looking you begin to see the world from the perspective of the other person, not just yourself."

"I guess I'm not built to trust employees."

"Isn't there anyone you really trust in your refinery?"

"Sure."

"Who?"

"Ann Laney."

"Are you sure?"

"What do you mean?" he countered. "I trust Ann Laney. She's terrific. She's tops. The office would fall apart without her. She keeps me straight on my diet. I'm almost embarrassed at times by the way she protects me and is loyal to me." He stopped, and shut his eyes. "Don't tell me I've messed up on Principle Four with Ann?"

"You do care about Ann," said the Woman in a consoling voice. "And you haven't messed up with her recently, but would you acknowledge that you often miss opportunities to make it better. For example, when you were in Europe for three weeks about a year ago, Ann took it upon herself to redecorate your office, something you have been wanting to do for years. Do you remember that?"

"Do I! I didn't recognize the place when I came back. She had changed the carpeting, wall coverings, furniture. The whole place was different."

"And you really appreciated what she had done, and you expressed your gratitude for her work, right?"

"Well, not exactly, at the time," said Harry offhandedly, as if he were conceding a small point. "I really didn't like the wild, explosive colors she picked out. And all the chrome edging on the tables, chairs, picture frames, desks, lamps, and the rest made the place look like a shiny Cadillac dealership. Besides, I felt she had overspent on furniture."

"So, you were actually upset with her?"

"I guess I was."

"If you recall, Harry, you expressed your dislike and displeasure quite vehemently at the time. But, isn't it also true that you are rather fond of your office now that you have grown accustomed to it?"

"It's turned out all right," he reluctantly agreed. "I've received a lot of compliments on it. To tell you the truth, everyone who comes in notices it and comments favorably on it."

"Why do you suppose Ann took it upon herself to redecorate your office?"

"Well, I suppose she thought it was something I wanted and that I would be surprised and pleased."

"Exactly," the Woman replied with relief. Her pupil had finally grasped an idea she was trying to teach. "And that's what I mean by loving intention. Ann's intention was to please you and to express her caring for you—her 'love' for you. And you didn't acknowledge that."

"You wouldn't want me to pretend I liked something when I didn't, would you?" he said sincerely.

"That's not the point, Harry," she explained. "Ann was doing her best to please you. You can acknowledge the goodness of her intention and praise her for it, even though you may not be altogether pleased with the outcome. Very few people operate out of evil motives or intentions. Most people do the best they know at the time. Their intentions are usually honorable, good, loving."

"So, how do I tell somebody like Ann, 'Thanks but no thanks'?"

"You do not have to agree with the outcome in order to acknowledge her good intention," replied the Woman. "For, example, you might have said, 'Ann, I'm overwhelmed by what you have done. It must have taken long hours to plan and carry out this project. You truly surprised me. I really appreciate the time and effort you put in to provide me with a redecorated office. Thank you so much.'"

"Now dismantle the whole thing, Ann, and put it back the way it was," he added sarcastically.

"You're lucky you really didn't say that to Ann, Harry," replied the Woman. "As it is, Ann's still not sure you appreciated her efforts. You've never told her so. As a matter of fact, she still feels as though she made a big mistake with the redecorations and is down on herself. On the other hand, if you had remembered to look for and acknowledge her loving intention at the time, it would have made her feel great and would have ensured you of continued acts of service above and beyond the call of duty."

"I guess you're right about that." Harry felt contrite. He knew he had missed it with Ann—a number of times. "What I'm beginning to see is that I haven't been expressing my appreciation for the efforts people are making. I've basically taken Ann's work for granted. I probably should pat her on the back more often."

"You might even enjoy it, Harry. And, just as a matter of course, you might enjoy looking for the good and loving intentions in what employees in general do, even when you yourself might have done it differently. It's kind of like those ties people give you at the holidays. You don't have to wear them to thank people for the loving intention in giving you the gift."

"I've never looked at it that way, but I guess the intention can be considered separately from the behavior. I've always focused on results—the final score—not the motivation behind the act. For me, whether or not employees were good was based only on the results they produced."

"If it's any comfort, you are not alone. It's a lesson many need to learn, not only at work but at home as well."

As Harry walked along a block of shops, she tested his comprehension of Principle Four.

"Harry, do you have any loving intentions?"

"What do you mean?"

"Are you in touch with having any loving intentions toward anyone, your wife, for example?"

"Sure, sure," answered Harry automatically, as he checked traffic and then crossed the street.

"Do you ever show those intentions?"

"Sure," he replied again.

"How? For example, do you demonstrate them in behavior?"

"What are you getting at?"

"If you, right now, got in touch with your loving intentions toward Molly and wanted to do something, what might you do?"

"What do you mean?" he asked, puzzled.

"Stop walking, Harry, and look."

At the moment, he was in front of a floral and gift shop.

"Any ideas?"

He looked into the window.

"Are you suggesting I get my wife some flowers?"

"Would that be something that might express your loving intentions toward Molly?"

"I hadn't thought of it," he replied honestly.

"If you were to get Molly some flowers, why would you do it?"

"I've never done it before," he replied sheepishly, "at least not since we've been married."

"I hear you saying you haven't indulged in feeling your own loving intentions for a long time. No wonder you find it hard to notice them in anyone else."

It took a few more minutes of coaching, but eventually Harry entered the shop, bought Molly a small bouquet of flowers, and proudly carried them home.

———————◆◆◆◆———————

At the front door of the Hartwell home, an astonished Molly stared at Harry's outstretched bouquet. When she was finally able to speak, she said: "Harry, are you feeling all right?" There was a note of concern in her voice because she knew he had been under a lot of strain these days.

"Why?"

"It's been at least twenty years since you brought me flowers." She blushed.

"I got in touch with my loving intention while I was walking home," he said matter-of-factly, as if he had been using the phrase all his life.

"Thank you," was all Molly could say. "Thank you for your loving intention. It's really nice."

"Yes, I was walking by the florist and something made me stop and go in, and here's what I chose for you."

She took the bouquet, smelled the flowers, and smiled. Then a puzzled look spread over her face. "What's going on with you, Harry? You've been quite different since your time in the hospital, and this bouquet really confirms it."

"What do you mean 'different'?" He knew he was improving in his heart-work with the Woman, but he wanted to hear someone say it, spell it out.

"You've been like a changed person. You've been listening and noticing. You've been gentle, too. I'm not as defensive around you. I like the change in you, Harry."

He welcomed the affirmation. He enjoyed knowing that someone else noticed.

Then, she added, "Is it something you really enjoy doing, I mean being gentle and loving?"

"I guess so." He wasn't too sure.

"How sweet you have become—after all these years."

He smiled.

She gave him a kiss and whispered in his ear, "Five minutes till dinner."

———————◆◆◆———————

He went into the bathroom to wash his hands, and looked into the mirror as he addressed the Woman. "If Molly knew this was my only alternative, she'd be doubly happy I'm changing."

"Why is that?" asked the Woman.

"I've got a gun at my head," he replied. "You should know, you're the one aiming it at me."

"Guns kill people, Harry. Managing from the heart is the only thing I want to put into your head. It never harmed anyone. In fact, it does just the opposite of what guns do. It brings life."

"Oh, you know what I mean when I say 'gun at my head,'" he replied. "You're holding the discretionary clock. It's Do or Die for me, right?"

"Where I come from," she replied, "we like to think of your discretionary training as 'Do and Live.'"

"Anyway," he said, "I'm glad Molly is noticing, and I'm glad she's pleased with my progress."

"I'm noticing, too, Harry," the Woman assured him, "and I'm pleased. It really takes very little to please people, if you say and do the right thing."

Harry smiled into the mirror. He, too, was pleased. It was like knowing the score at half-time, knowing your team was ahead.

"It's easy to find the loving intention of somebody who agrees with you," she continued, "but much harder when they don't. The big challenge comes when you are able to find the loving intention of somebody who disagrees with you."

"You mean like Jim Weiss?" said Harry, checking to see that he had caught the Woman's point.

She agreed.

"I remember being in your shiny white room when you first told me this fourth principle," he reminisced, "and you offered me a thousand dollars if I could find a loving intention behind Jim's harebrained scheme for weekly meetings."

As he switched off the bathroom light, he heard the Woman say, "Let me give you fair warning that Principle Four will be up for testing tomorrow. Be ready for it."

———————◆◖◗◆————————

Harry was conducting the refinery's budget meeting in the Ramoco Board Room with its classic brown leather chairs. Nobody enjoyed budget meetings, even in comfortable chairs. And, in the intensity of the meeting, Harry forgot about loving intentions, as soon as Jim Weiss stood up to make a presentation, holding forth with 'another harebrained idea,' Merit Pay for Teams.

"I've been studying different ways of rewarding outstanding performance," Jim explained. "And I'd like to toss this idea around with you for a few minutes. It looks like research shows that the most effective way is to reward the team for its collective performance rather than a single employee for individual performance."

"Jim, wait a minute!" burst in Harry. "I don't care what research shows. In this refinery, we give awards only to stars, not to those who hitch a free ride on the efforts of others." Harry looked around the room, visually collecting signs of approval for what he had just said, then he addressed Jim directly. "Look at it logically. If I get paid on the volume of refined products I produce, why in the world should I help you if it reduces my production?"

A few of the others grunted in reply to Harry's question, as if it was a point that Jim Weiss needed to deal with.

Jim winced at Harry's interruption, took a deep breath, and went on. "The fact is that research shows that giving individuals rewards produces a few happy individuals, but a lot of jealous, annoyed co-workers."

"So?" challenged Harry, smirking, again looking around for nods of approval. "Let the lazy ones stew in their jealousy, or invite them to work their butts off and see how easy it is to win the Most Valuable Player award."

Jim had expected some resistance from Harry, so he had come well-prepared. He took another deep breath and countered. "Team awards get everyone on a team to do well. Group-based incentives encourage cooperation, not competition and rivalry."

"Maybe you're just too young in business, Jim," said Harry, "to realize that freeloaders will freeload. Your suggestion merely helps them enjoy rewards they don't deserve."

"But look at this situation from a team's perspective," argued Jim. "In order to get their group reward, the other team members will get the freeloader to improve, to contribute to the success of the team."

Harry stood up to speak. He was a head taller than Jim Weiss.

Jim heard the unspoken order to sit down. He sat.

"America became the most powerful country in the world through rugged individualism," said Harry definitively, "and that's the way my refinery is going to make it to the top."

He surveyed the faces in the room again, then sat down, thinking he had administered the final swat to Jim's ill-fated idea.

But Jim and his idea were still very much alive. Jim got up and began again.

"When I called Ramoco headquarters to see if this idea was in line with corporate policy," Jim said, "Carl Harris told me he was considering Merit Rewards for Teams very seriously across the U.S. Area."

"Let's leave Accounting out of this," said Harry, dismissing Carl Harris. "They count dollar bills. They know nothing about oil production and on-line performance."

"But, Harry," said Jim, "isn't the writing on the wall already? At Ramoco our shift to high tech is requiring higher and higher levels of teamwork. It's only natural to reward the teams we're trying to build."

Some of those at the meeting were listening more attentively than before to Jim Weiss, but Harry had had enough of Jim's idea. He stood up authoritatively and called for a coffee break.

———◆◆◆———

"Harry, you're doing it again," came the Woman's kindly voice, as he stepped into his own office. "I know it seems remote to you, but could Jim Weiss possibly have a loving intention in his proposal?"

"Get off my back." He turned to face the window and looked outside.

"I asked you, Harry," she gently insisted, "could Jim have a positive intention?"

"If he does, it's not obvious to me."

"Look again, Harry," she encouraged. "Look harder."

"Well, I guess he could have one," he suggested, but not very convincingly.

"Find it, Harry," she urged him, "and acknowledge it, because the discretionary clock is ticking away."

It took only a few moments of reflection to find a good intention. He turned around and told it to her.

"Great, Harry! We're on our way."

As Harry stood near his desk, the Woman coached him on how to bring up the good intention and affirm it. Together they rehearsed how Harry could talk to Jim Weiss when the meeting resumed.

"Regardless of how wild an idea may sound, Harry," she said, "when you dig to find its author's loving intention, you usually find something about the idea that you can use productively."

———————◆◆◆———————

Back in the Board Room, Harry began by addressing Jim Weiss.

"Let me see if I can get to your intention, Jim. As I see it, you want to find a way to get workers to cooperate more than they do now, and to develop a sense of teamwork."

Jim nodded, surprised to hear such non-rejecting words coming from Harry.

"You feel that if we reward teamwork," continued Harry, "the top performers will help bring others up to speed, right?"

"Right, Harry," replied Jim with enthusiasm. "And not only that. The beauty of team merit is that instead of only one team winning the merit incentive, as many teams can win as meet the performance criteria. We don't have to give out only one award, we can give out eight of them."

"How are we going to measure results or set criteria?" asked Harry.

"We don't have to dream up criteria for each group. Let the teams themselves come up with some proposals of their own. Let them create their own standards. And if we find that they're setting goals too low, we can adjust them."

"I'm still concerned about the freeloaders, Jim, and I think some of the others are, too."

A number of the group agreed. The freeloaders were still an unresolved issue.

"In this merit system," explained Jim, "it's the teams that are rewarded. It's the team's task to confront freeloaders and bring their performance up to par. Each team will solve that problem in its own way. What we in management have to do is to create a structure that gives teams a high incentive to confront their members with performance problems."

"That should be pretty easy," said Harry with genuine approval. "I'm glad that you've thought your idea all the way through, Jim. I believe you're really dedicated to finding ways to improve everyone's performance."

"Thanks for hanging in there with me," said Jim with a big smile.

Looking around the meeting table, Harry observed that most of the others were liking Jim Weiss' idea. Much as he hated to admit it, so was he.

"Not only that," continued Jim with a newfound excitement, "you'll develop the kind of team commitment and enthusiasm they have in major league baseball."

"And you're saying," said Harry, doing a Listening Check, "that we can give out pennants to every team that meets an established standard? That we might eventually produce a whole refinery full of winning teams? That's your vision, isn't it?"

"Exactly."

———————◆◗◖◆◗◆—————

"I just realized," he said silently to the Woman, "that if I hadn't been working on Principle Four today, I would have blown Weiss' great idea away. I wouldn't even have considered it."

"The good news, Harry, is that you did consider it. When you went looking for a loving intention, you found a great idea. Not only is Jim Weiss tickled, but that new idea is going to have a bottom-line impact on your refinery. And that should make you happy."

He grinned.

———————◆◗◖◆◗◆—————

At noon, Harry Hartwell and Neil Curtis were having lunch in the refinery cafeteria.

As Vice President for Human Resources from Ramoco headquarters, Neil Curtis preferred to eat lunch surrounded by the other refinery employees. He was always watching and observing. He found that, when people were eating, they were usually honest in their praise as well as in their criticism.

"I like to listen to our people in a nonthreatening setting," was the way Curtis put it.

The Woman reminded Harry of Neil Curtis, who often seemed to be promoting stuff like caring about people, their feelings, and intentions.

Harry had just emerged from his budget meeting and was still spinning with what had happened there. He had started out by condemning Jim Weiss' proposal, but had left the meeting a convert to Merit Rewards for Teams. He was explaining to Neil how looking for loving intentions had brought about his change of mind toward Jim Weiss and his idea.

"It's amazing what an effect it has on people to publicly affirm their positive intentions," Harry explained. "As soon as I said what I thought his true intentions were, Jim stopped trying to defend his position and simply shared his excitement with us about the plan. And once I began really acknowledging his loving intentions, even I started to see his idea differently."

"Did someone at headquarters tell you about loving intentions?" asked Neil. "Is that where you picked up the idea?"

"Why would you think that?" asked Harry cagily. He had never told anyone about the Woman who was coaching him through his discretionary period.

"We sometimes do Loving Intentions during our Human Resources staff meetings at headquarters."

"You what?" said Harry incredulously.

"Yes, we do," said Neil. "In fact, we invoke a Loving Intentions Rule at these meetings whenever things get too tense."

"How do you do it?" asked Harry, his eyes wide open. He wondered, but didn't dare to ask, if the Woman had coached someone beside himself at Ramoco.

"When people at a staff meeting get overly contentious," explained Neil, "we impose the Loving Intention Rule. It means that before you can disagree with someone, you are required to come up with a statement about that person's loving intention. You say: 'After reflecting on the point you just made, I think your loving intention is to . . .' Everybody keeps stating the loving intentions of others until we've all gotten back to thinking like a team."

"I guess it's pretty hard to get mad at a person who's just acknowledged your good intentions," said Harry.

"Right," Neil agreed. "Since we continue to treat each other with respect, it makes for a productive and supportive meeting."

"Neil, do you people at corporate headquarters really practice that Loving Intention Rule, or are you pulling my leg?"

"Scout's honor, Harry. At least the Human Resources staff."

"Doesn't it take up a lot of time?"

"Not really. In the long run, it takes less time to conclude a successful meeting using the Loving Intention Rule, because people aren't at odds with one another. They're not at each other's throats. Instead of attributing enemy motives to staff members, you presume the other person is committed to working for the betterment of the team."

"The way I did with Jim Weiss?"

"Exactly."

—————— ◆◦◆ ——————

"**I** was rather taken by surprise at lunch today," said Harry to the Woman. "I thought your principles for managing from the heart were something heavenly, but old Neil Curtis knew all about them."

"Harry, managing from the heart is not something we invented last month as a tool to torment you. Managing from the heart is not new. It is a natural way for humans to be, except when they're fearful. When people are fearful and insecure, they can't act naturally. This principle of Loving Intentions has always been around. Some people discover it and find it a natural way to operate. You found it unnatural."

"Do you think it will ever become second-nature to me?"

"I'm certainly counting on it," concluded the Woman.

---◆◆◆---

"Acknowledge The Greatness Within Me"

---◆◆◆---

It was a shimmering, clear May evening, but Harry didn't notice the setting sun or the early red azaleas in bloom as he stomped along the path. He tugged at the sleeve of his raggedy old brown cardigan, and snorted.

"You're angry for sure tonight," said the Woman, "but your anger seems to be a sign of something deeper. What is it, Harry?" She waited for an answer.

He sighed deeply. It was hard for him to recall a time when the Woman who seemed to live inside him hadn't been his constant companion.

"I'm really disappointed in my son, Bob. He came home from school today to fight with me for his next semester's tuition. His grade point average is still 2.25. I *know* he's brighter than that. And even though I'm disappointed about his low grades, I'm really angry with him. I'd like to cut him down to size for goofing off. I'd like to do something drastic to get him to wake up—like throw him out of the house." Harry clenched his fist and shook his arm as he remembered the scene he had just left.

Bob had gotten up from the dining room table and gone into the family room. He sat on the sofa, picked up the remote control for the television set, and clicked it until he found a sitcom to watch.

His father had followed him into the family room and sat down on his easy chair. He picked up the morning newspaper, opened it, looked at it for a few minutes, then folded it and put it down. He looked at Bob quietly for a few seconds, then addressed him, speaking above the volume of the television program.

"How come you didn't do very well this semester, Bob?" Harry began in a genuine attempt to listen with understanding and to look for Bob's loving intentions.

Although Bob didn't take his eyes from the television screen, he had been prepared for that inevitable question, and answered: "For one thing, I took a physics course and I had no idea the labs would take up so much time." Then, turning to face his father, he added, "I also went out for soccer. Afternoon practice almost every day took a lot of time."

"So, you found the physics labs too time-consuming and soccer ate up the rest of your study time?" Harry was secretly disappointed that Bob had chosen soccer over football.

Bob's attention returned to the screen. "I did get a letter in soccer. I thought you'd be happy to know that."

"That's an accomplishment. But, would you say that soccer was enough to wipe out every night's study time?" Harry was looking at Bob, who seemed to be absorbed in the sitcom.

"Well, I also broke up with Jeanne this semester," he said, turning to face his father for a moment, "and I'm really sad about that."

"You're missing her, and I'll bet that's depressing," said Harry. "My guess is that studying or grades is not the most important part of your life right now."

"That's right. And, dad?"

"Yes?"

"I'm thinking of changing my major from chemistry to history. I'm finding science very tough. I think, with history or something easy like that, it would be smooth sailing for me."

Harry stood up, walked to the window, and looked out. "Sounds like you're not sure yet what you really want, but you are sure that, whatever you choose to major in this time around, it ought to be easy."

"That's right. Besides, dad, don't you think I ought to really enjoy my college years?"

"I think it's great to have fun now and then, but fun is not really the major objective of a college education." He was still looking out the window.

"I know that. But college is sort of my last fling before I have to face the real world."

Harry turned to face him. "Do you see your mother and me as having agreed to support four years of fling?" His voice had an edge to it.

"You know what I mean, dad," he said, sitting up, facing his father, and smiling.

"Maybe you have the best of intentions, Bob," he sighed. "But I'm having a hard time discerning them. Could you clarify things a bit for me?"

"Well, I guess I want to do well in school and also enjoy myself. I don't think that's too much to ask."

"Do you have any concrete plans for achieving success in school?"

"I told you that I would probably change my major to history. That's one plan."

"Will that help you achieve success, or just make things easier?"

"Well, at least I'll be able to get a 2.5 and still enjoy life a bit."

"Do you really like history?"

"I guess it's okay." His eyes were pulled back to the television screen.

"Would it be a field you'd like to develop a career in?" Harry's voice became more insistent, and he began walking toward the sofa where Bob was sitting.

Bob turned his head as Harry approached. "I really haven't thought about it that much, dad."

"I wish you would. And it's about time you did," said Harry, coldly. "If you expect me to support you, I want to be sure my investment will be put to good use. I want to get my money's worth out of your tuition."

With that, Harry hurried out of the room. "It's time for my walk," he muttered. In a few moments, the front door slammed and Harry had left the house.

———— ◆◈◆ ————

"**Y**ou really are disappointed in him, aren't you?" the Woman reflected.

"It's the same old story with Bob—plenty of potential but little commitment. No real effort. He could top 2.5 easily if he only put his mind to it. I guess I've been putting up with his lack of all-out effort for years, and now I'm sick and tired of it."

"You had big expectations for him, and he hasn't fulfilled the highest of them?"

"I had every right to those expectations," insisted Harry. "While I'm out walking for the next hour, he'll sweet-talk his mother about next semester's tuition and get her to take his side. When I walk back in the house, he'll be all full of apologies for not doing better, as always. But I'll bet my Chrysler that he'll be back at the end of next semester with the same old mediocre grades and the same old sob story—apologies, promises, sweet talk."

"Harry, it sounds like you and Bob are in a stuck place, and you don't know what to do to get out of it."

"That's why I left the house just now, claiming I had to take my heart-building walk. I didn't want to blow up at him. He may be smart enough to get accepted into college, but if he was an employee of mine and performed like that, I would probably can him. But how can you fire your own son?"

The Woman spoke gently. "Is he really all that worthless, dispensable, replaceable?"

"No," he said, shoving his hands in his pockets. "I love him. He's my own flesh and blood. But, damn, I get frustrated with him and the way he is wasting his talents and his life."

"Do you think Bob knows you love him and value him as much as you do?" she asked.

"Who can know what goes on in his mind?" he snapped angrily. "He certainly doesn't see me as valuable, except as his checkbook to college."

"Harry," she replied tenderly, "I think it's a good time for us to look at Principle Five. Do you remember it?"

"I can't remember anything now," he said, dejected.

"Principle Five says that when people look at you they silently say, *Acknowledge the greatness within me*."

Harry was silent as he crossed at the intersection. Even the birds had stopped their chirping.

"What's that principle got to do with Bob and me?" he finally asked. "I don't see the connection. How do I acknowledge his greatness when I don't have anything to acknowledge?"

"Harry, right now you are so locked into his 2.25 grade point average that you can't see anything else."

"What else do you want me to see?" he asked.

"Shift gears, Harry," she said. "I invite you to step out of your critical mind and begin looking at Bob from your compassionate heart. Let your heart see your son's preciousness, his untapped potential. What he *could* do, not what he has failed to do. Can you remember a time when you had dreams for him?"

The Woman's presence felt soothing to Harry. Some of his emotional ice was beginning to melt.

"Sure, I remember," he replied, his voice still echoing disappointment. "All his life I had dreams for him. I envisioned him doing great things. He's a handsome kid, good in sports, got a sharp mind, people love him, a real extrovert. He could do anything he put his mind to."

"Did you ever think or dream about Bob's uniqueness," she suggested, "how there was no one else quite like him? Did you think of what he could contribute to the world?"

"Sure," he replied, not knowing where the conversation was heading. "He has the makings of a great businessman, a great lawyer, a great manager—if only he would apply himself. That's what I used to say to his mother all the time. I used to stand next to her and smile at Bob and say, 'Our kid will be great someday.'"

"You know what?" began the Woman. "I think Bob has no idea you hold him in such high regard. I suspect that if you were to review the personal conversations you and Bob have had since he started college, there would not be very many times when you acknowledged the greatness within him, the way you're doing now."

"I guess I've spent most of those conversations grousing about his poor grades."

"This principle is not about grades but about potential. Potential means something that hasn't fully come to light. It's about the greatness *within*. It's something in Bob that's still waiting to be called forth."

"Untapped potential?" asked Harry, who was finally beginning to hear her idea above the noise of his anger and sadness.

"Right," she replied. "You need to find a way not to dump on Bob, but to help him value himself, to call forth his own belief in himself. If he knows that you truly want him to live to his highest potential and that you believe in him, maybe he can learn to want it enough to make it happen. Perhaps, if he felt your support in that choice, he himself would make the commitment to school and put in the necessary effort to succeed. Everyone has his or her own greatness and that greatness longs to be acknowledged."

"I'm not sure what you mean by greatness," he broke in. "That's a term I have always reserved for a select group of people." He paused, then went on. "I certainly don't think I'm great."

"Of course, you have greatness in you, Harry," she said. "Everyone has a unique greatness. But for most people, it remains an untapped potential. I'm talking about the potential they have but of which they are unaware. Can you recall, over the years, people whom you knew could achieve at a much higher level, but for one reason or another never quite made it?"

"You know, that has always frustrated me. I've always thought of myself as a good judge of character, but some of the people I've put my money on just never lived up to expectations. That's what I fear about Bob, that he's never going to reach his potential."

"What kinds of expectations does Bob have of himself?"

"He's never talked much about them to me. I guess I really don't know. Maybe he really doesn't have any."

"Sometimes people need someone else to name the greatness inside them. Isn't that how you got started?"

"I don't understand."

"Think back when you first went to work for Ramoco," she began. "Do you remember your first boss?"

"I certainly do." He smiled for the first time that evening.

Just then, a bird began chirping. Soon, another bird joined in and, before long, the entire flock was chattering.

"It was Hugh Powell," he continued, "one of the finest men I have ever known. I still think of him often and wish he were around so I could talk with him."

"Remember the time you were so discouraged you were about to quit Ramoco?"

Harry nodded.

"You had been given your first promotion," she said. "As a new manager you were received with something less than enthusiasm by your subordinates. Some of the older ones who had been bypassed for promotion resented you and took every opportunity to let you know that they had more experience on the job than you, and implied that they could make you or break you."

"Yes, I remember," he replied, reliving for a moment the pain that those older men had caused him to feel. "I was so frustrated and angry. I couldn't seem to get those guys excited to go for the goals I had set. Nothing I said or did seemed to work. I was sure I was headed for the first major defeat of my career. I was almost paralyzed by fear of failure, and nearly panicked."

"And it was Hugh who got you back on track," said the Woman. "Do you remember how he talked to you?"

"Well, he wasn't easy on me but he helped me get my mind focused. He made me look at my past accomplishments and affirm my strengths, and then he said something I'll never forget. He said, 'Harry, you're immensely talented and I predict you're going to be a giant in this corporation. You just need the courage to believe in yourself.'"

"That's Principle Five at work, Harry," she said. "Hugh Powell was an expert in managing from the heart."

"I felt nine feet tall when I left that meeting, and I've reminded myself of that conversation many times over the years."

"Hugh acknowledged your greatness," she explained. "It was hidden inside you, and he saw it and affirmed it. You have had opportunities to pass Hugh's gift along many times, but for some reason you seldom did it."

"I guess I just don't remember those times." Harry's mind went blank, as a way to avoid an unwelcome memory. "When, for example, did I mess up on this principle?"

"Do you remember when Joe Marek was one of the candidates for promotion to the refinery personnel manager's job?"

"Yes, I remember," he replied. "He lost out to Denise Wong, who was the sharpest and most effective person I had ever seen in that function. I felt Denise was more qualified for the job, and that's what I told Joe when I made the assignment. I was very honest and up front with him."

"That's right," agreed the Woman. "But what you don't know is how devastated he felt to be passed over."

"But that's the name of the game," he replied. "There are always more people than slots to fill. My job is to make tough decisions. I don't enjoy delivering bad news."

"I'm sure you don't," she acknowledged. "And I also know you have a very high regard for Joe. Except that Joe doesn't know it! He needed you that day, to do for him what Hugh did for you—affirm the greatness, the potential you saw in him. Your affirmation at the time may not have made the decision any easier for him to digest, but it would have nourished him to keep going and keep growing and be ready when the next opening came up."

"I guess you're right. I do like Joe and want him to succeed. He has a lot to offer Ramoco." Then he added, "In fact, he does remind me a lot of myself at his age."

"All the Joes hope they have potential greatness. They carry that hope around in their hearts like a little plant. When somebody else sees it and mentions it, it's like pouring water on the plant to make it grow. When you affirm the greatness inside people, you empower them. They stand straighter. They walk taller."

Harry nodded.

"So now you know what I mean by acknowledging greatness." said the Woman.

"Yes, I do, and you're right."

"Good, Harry. I'm proud of you."

"But I don't know if I can really do it with Bob. Tonight, I mean. I'm still feeling angry at him."

"That's okay," said the Woman. "Bob can accept that. He's probably angry and disappointed at himself. He won't be surprised to know that you're also feeling this way. In fact, he'd be surprised if you weren't."

"Oh, here's the floral shop," he said. "I'm going to stop in and get some roses for Molly. She loves roses, you know."

———————◆■◆———————

An hour ago, when Harry had walked out of his home in silence, he left a lot of tension behind. Molly and Bob were sure that a storm was brewing. Seated in the living room, mother and son discussed college tuition as they waited for Harry's return.

"Mom, you've got to help me," he pleaded. "The way dad went out of here, he was ready to chew my head off."

"Your father gets angry regularly," she said, smiling, "and you know your grades are a sore spot with him."

"2.25 is not bad."

"That's not the point, Bob." She shook her head emphatically as she looked at him. "Last year, the three of us made an agreement about tuition and grades. And you have not kept your part. To your father and me, agreements are very important. I can tell you that everything in the real estate business is based on people keeping their word."

"This is a big year coming up at school, and I need to know that you'll be behind me when dad comes back."

"Last semester when you didn't make the agreed-upon grade," his mother began, "you begged me not to cut off your money supply."

"It'll be different this time." He looked directly into Molly's eyes.

"That's what you said last semester, Bob, so I went over his head and had to deal with his anger for signing that tuition check."

"I had a bunch of professors who were stingy with grades, so I didn't get the grade point average I deserved."

"But you still didn't keep your agreement, and I'm angry and hurt about that."

"Other things came up, mom."

"I'm sure they did." she said, "They always do, Bob, for all of us. The question is: Which things take first place for you?"

"College is important to me, mom, so please get dad to pay my tuition."

"I love you, Bob, and I want you to succeed." She reached over to touch him. "And you may feel cheated by your professors, but this time around you're on your own with dad. You're going to have to deal with him by yourself."

"But, mom, you're my one hope."

"Perhaps you can convince your father to give you a third chance."

"But you know how he is when he's angry."

"I'm not surprised that you're scared to face your father. He is kind of threatening. If anyone knows that side of him, I do. But you also know that he loves you."

"Are you telling me you won't support me?"

"I'm telling you he loves you and wants the best for you. You may not see him that way at this moment." Then, she added, "And neither of us can predict the mood he'll be in when he gets back from his walk."

"Yeah," nodded Bob. "I'll bet he'd like to bash my head in."

When the back door opened a few seconds later, the two of them jumped defensively, looked at each other, and nervously moved toward the kitchen. Mother and son stood silently expectant.

"Roses for you, my darling Molly," said Harry with a smile, bringing the bouquet from behind his back.

Surprised at his behavior, Molly moved forward, took the flowers, and gave Harry a kiss. "How thoughtful," she said.

"You have always wanted the best for our family," he replied. "Even when I have forgotten it, you haven't. I love you for that. No amount of flowers could ever repay your constancy."

This was most unexpected language coming from the Harry that had fumed his way out the door an hour ago.

"Thank you, Harry," she said, standing close to him and reaching out to touch his face. "Those words mean so much coming from you."

It was an awkward moment for all of them.

This time Molly took the lead. "Harry, the matter of Bob's tuition is still unsettled."

"That's right," said Harry looking directly into Molly's eyes. "But first, I have something to talk to Bob about, man-to-man, something that is more important than tuition."

Bob couldn't imagine what that could be.

In the study, Harry and Bob sat face to face.

Bob was still confused, so he decided to listen, at least until he could figure out what was on his father's mind.

"The reason I went out for my walk when I did," Harry began, "was because I refused to say to you that your 2.25 average was okay with me."

"But, dad," Bob interrupted, anxious and eager to defend himself, "last semester I had exactly the same average and mom paid my tuition then. Why isn't it okay now?"

"I repeat, 2.25 is not okay with me." Then, looking Bob in the eye and with a tinge of sadness, he added, "I wish it wasn't okay with you either."

He waited a moment and then went on.

"To me, what's more important than your grade point average is the fact that the poor average you got is apparently okay with you."

"Dad, grades aren't everything."

"No, they aren't," Harry agreed. "But they are a *sign* of certain things."

Bob remained silent.

"As I look at you," Harry began, "I see a potentially great student. You have a brilliant mind. But I believe you're playing the game of college with one hand tied behind your back. You're not really playing flat out. Do you remember when you and I used to play one-on-one basketball in the back yard?"

Bob nodded.

"You would go all out to get the ball from me. You'd even throw an elbow in your old man's ribs just to get a rebound. You practiced your jump shot hour after hour, just so you could beat me. That's the kind of effort I'm talking about. That's the kind of effort I'm looking for from you in your education. You and I both know you have a wonderful mind. If, at school, you gave close to the effort you used to give playing basketball, we wouldn't have to be discussing tuition now."

"Do *you* really think I can make the grade?"

Harry was stunned. It was the first time he'd realized that his own son didn't know how highly he valued him. "I sure do," he said. "Your mom and I have always said that you're the one with brains in our family. You are going to be a great man someday. All the potential you need to be great is already inside you."

"I'm really sorry about the low grade point average this semester, dad."

"I am, too, especially since I know the kind of drive you're capable of. I don't expect you to be the best in your class, but I do expect you to do your best."

Bob was silent.

"Do you agree with me that you weren't doing your best these last two semesters?"

"I'm going to do my best this semester, dad, I promise."

"That's good, Bob. I'm honored that you would make that promise to me. I will take you at your word. And I will do what I can to help you keep that promise."

"Thanks, dad."

Bob got up to go. Dad will now shake my hand, he thought, tell me I have one more chance, and promise to put the tuition check in the mail Monday morning.

But Harry hadn't gotten to his main point of acknowledging Bob's greatness. "Bob," he said, "the promise you just made to me is important, but it's more important for you to make that promise to yourself, because your hard work this coming semester will earn your tuition from me for the following semester."

To Bob, his father's words sounded like double talk.

"You *will* pay my way this semester, won't you, dad," Bob asked, "like you and mom did last semester?"

Harry realized Bob had missed his point, and that Bob was still playing the game of What-do-I-have-to-do-to-get-dad-to-pay-my-tuition?

"I'm on your side, Bob," he began again. "I won't settle for less than your best. It's not a matter of grades, though grades happen to be the issue at the moment. If I believe in your potential greatness, and I do," he continued slowly, emphasizing every word, "I won't support your halfhearted efforts. But I will support your wholehearted efforts. This semester you are on your own financially. But, more importantly, this semester I am being true to my promise in calling you to live up to the potential that is within you."

"I'm not sure I understand what you're getting at, dad."

"Bob, you are a bright star, shining with talent, skill, personality, savvy. As soon as you begin studying with the effort and determination you used to put into beating me in one-on-one basketball, your grades will climb far beyond a 2.5. But I want you to do it for *you,* for all that waits inside you. I want you to take responsibility for yourself in this matter. When you bring home a 2.5 or higher, the ticket for your education will be on me. It will be my pleasure. I'll be proud to support you financially."

Bob shuffled uncomfortably on the sofa. The content and delivery of the words he was hearing were most unlike his father, a total change. It was so silent in the room that they could both hear the second-by-second click of the quartz clock on the desk nearby.

"You're right about the basketball stuff, dad," said Bob finally, "but how am I going to come up with the bread to pay tuition?"

"I believe in you," said Harry, staying focused on his son's potential greatness. "You just need the courage to believe in yourself." He was surprised at how right those words sounded, those exact words that Hugh Powell has spoken to him many years ago.

"Are you saying that you are cutting me off?" His mouth opened in surprise. "What did I do to deserve that?"

"If you're worried about money, Bob, you have a few basic options. For example, you can try working on top of a full class load, you can attend school part-time and work the rest, you can apply for a student loan, or you can work for a year and then go back to college. As I recall, you also have some savings. I expect you'll use your talents, brains, and strength to come up with whatever you need for tuition."

With hands folded and head bent forward, Bob looked penitent on the outside, but Harry suspected that, as a Hartwell, there must be some anger behind his son's apologetic look.

"Right now, you may be angry at me for what seems to you my lack of support. But I am on your side, truly I am. I would not be true to myself or to you if I were to capitulate and say, 'What the heck, I'll pay his tuition no matter what.' The only thing I will do 'no matter what' is believe in you. I want you to be proud of who you are and what you accomplish in life. I will not contribute to mediocre performance, especially since I know how much more you are capable of giving. I challenge you to take responsibility for your life."

Bob was silent. On one level, he was angry and confused because he would have to earn his own way to stay in college another semester. On another level, he was proud that his father loved and valued him so highly, believed in him so thoroughly, and would name his academic performance for exactly what it was.

Bob raised his head to meet his father's eyes. "I guess I made an agreement with you and mom, and I haven't lived up to it. That's the bottom line, isn't it?"

Harry nodded and smiled, but the smile was bittersweet.

"You wouldn't consider giving me a loan to cover my tuition, would you?"

"Your mother and I won't renege on our part of the agreement."

"I guess that means No."

Harry extended his hand toward his son. Bob looked at the proffered hand, thought about it for a moment, then took it. "Well, it's time for me to get back to school and begin looking for a job."

"Before you leave, Bob," Harry said, "be sure to tell your mother that, from now on, you are accepting responsibility for your own life."

———◆◆◆◆———

When Harry arrived at his office a few days later, he had another opportunity to practice Principle Five.

A distraught Hector Morales, head of purchasing at the refinery, knocked on Harry's door, came in, walked over to his desk, and silently handed him a letter of resignation.

"What is this all about?" asked Harry, looking up at the younger man.

Hector said nothing, his shoulders stooped, hands hanging limply by his sides.

Some months ago, Hector had made a hefty purchase of crude from the Saudis at what he thought was the lowest price. But instead of rising, prices continued to fall. They continued downward for the next six months. And Hector was very embarrassed and distraught to have saddled Ramoco with a monumental inventory, priced well over the current market. And, as far as he was concerned, it was all his fault.

That was a terrible burden for a proud man to bear, so Hector decided the only noble thing to do would be to disappear from Ramoco.

Harry read Hector's letter of resignation, then he looked up at the young man.

"Let me see if I understand what's going on," Harry began calmly. "A decision you strongly recommended to me and then implemented cost the company about $10 million. You had sensed a trend and bought on that trend. But you were too right because the trend continued, and you got us into an overcommitted position. Now, because you misjudged an opportunity, you're humiliated and want to quit. Is that the sum and substance of it?"

"Yeah, boss," said Hector. "That's the story in a nutshell. I blew it big-time."

"Your resignation is not accepted," said Harry and he tore up Hector's letter. "Now, let's sit down and talk about it," he said, taking charge of the meeting.

Harry sat there like a football coach with the team on Monday morning reviewing videotapes of yesterday's losing game.

"Look, Hector," he began. "In the first place, I wouldn't let you go over to the competition for any amount of money. You're too valuable to me. Furthermore, you cannot take sole responsibility for this mistake. I approved the purchase. More importantly, you were the first to get wind of the downturn. That was good. You correctly spotted the downward movement in oil prices before anybody else did. That was valuable. You saw it before it came over the horizon. That was terrific. You just didn't know *how* right you were going to be. Hector, it's not your responsibility that the Saudis kept dumping crude after that initial period."

"But I overcommitted us. A good purchasing man would have left room for flexibility, and I didn't."

"Morales," Harry said, "I consider you a genius in purchasing. You consistently get us the best deals, and you have a great nose for the future. This one time you were unlucky and you were *too* right. It could have gone the other way. The Saudis could have curtailed production, and we would have been sitting pretty. Besides, you know as well as I that our prices are averaged out so that lumps like this one get smoothed over."

"But it really was my fault," Hector insisted. "I didn't see the shift quickly enough."

"Forgive yourself, Hector, for not being psychic," he said. "And if you need my forgiveness for taking this risk and committing our company for too much too early, you have it."

Hector smiled.

"In the long run," Harry added, "we're really no worse off than the other U.S. oil companies."

"Really, boss?"

"Regardless of the outcome of this transaction, I consider you a star in our company. I would no more let you go to another team than the old Yankees would have traded Joe DiMaggio."

"Really, boss?" said Hector again. "You'd compare me to DiMaggio?"

"You're by far the best purchasing agent I've ever seen. You're young and smart, and you're going to have a great career in this company."

"Boss, I didn't know you really felt that way about me. I didn't know you liked me that much. I thought it was all over for me here at Ramoco. You know, I really am sorry about overpurchasing all that oil."

"Forget it, Hector," said Harry, as he gave the young man a big bear hug. "Those things happen all the time." Then, giving Hector a friendly shove toward the door, he added laughingly, "Now, get back to work."

———— ◆◆◆ ————

"Whew," exclaimed Harry to the Woman, as soon as Hector left the office. "That was a close call."

"You really let him know how valuable he was to you and the company, Harry," she said.

"He sure is valuable and I sure let him know it," said Harry, "and I'm glad I did. If that kid had walked out of here today, the competition would have snapped him up in a minute."

"Thanks to you recognizing his greatness," she added, "he walked out of your office with a smile."

"I simply let him know he was deeply appreciated by me. After all, I don't know any other purchasing agents who have the nose of a futures trader."

"Harry, I think you've learned to use this principle well. You didn't need help today at all."

"Amen," he said. "What's next on the agenda?"

"What you would call a final exam," replied the Woman. "You've proved to me that you have learned each of the five principles of managing from the heart. Whenever you've failed to implement any of the principles, you were able to redeem yourself within twenty-four hours."

Harry beamed.

"Next," she continued, "in a few days, you will have a final test which will require you to use all five principles with one person during a single session. If you are successful, you will win complete discretion. No more tests. No more deadlines. No more me. You'll be back on your own. You'll be the only one responsible for your life. You can decide for yourself, then, how you want to manage yourself and others."

Six months ago, those words would have been the sweetest sounds Harry could have ever heard coming from the Woman. Right now, Harry wasn't so sure how he felt about her words.

Harry's Final Exam

It had rained all night so the streets were slippery and the commuters were surly on their way to work this Monday morning. However, Harry Hartwell's attention was not on the weather nor the traffic. He was focused on today's upcoming Board of Director's meeting, which could be the most important meeting of his career.

Driving to headquarters, he thought back over his career with Ramoco. He began right out of college, just a few years older than his son was right now. His first job was inspector on the fractionator. From the inspector's job, he was promoted, in turn, to supervisor, foreman, operations supervisor, assistant refinery manager, and finally, three years ago, to refinery manager. That was as far up as he could climb in this location.

Today's meeting was the opportunity Harry had been dreaming of. The current Vice President in charge of all U.S. Operations, Rudolph Garrett, had just announced his retirement date, and J. Lawrence Babcock, Jr., Ramoco's CEO, affectionately known as Sir Lawrence, was soon to announce Garrett's successor. If Harry looked good during his presentation today, he felt it would make the promotion a shoo-in.

Harry believed he had only one competitor for the U.S. Operations position, Carl Harris. At least, that's the way rumor had it. But Harry wasn't really sure Carl wanted the job. One was never quite sure what Carl wanted. As Vice President in charge of Finance, Carl's office was at headquarters, no more than a first-down away from Sir Lawrence's desk, far across town from Harry's refinery. While Harry seldom got a chance to show his stuff in front of the CEO, Carl could have Babcock's ear any time he wanted it. What he whispered in that ear, no one knew.

Carl had never come out openly jockeying for the U.S. Operations position.

"You would think he'd be happy enough managing all the Ramoco money," Harry used to say.

He and Carl were not close, to put it mildly, and Carl was not very open with him, or with anybody else, as far as he could tell.

Harry was a competitor, a fighter. And today were the play-offs. He abhorred the thought of losing. He liked to feel proud of himself, and he always liked others to be proud of him, too, especially his father, when he was alive. Even though Harry had made the football team at Duke and followed in his father's footsteps at Ramoco, his father never talked about Harry's greatness. And so Harry always questioned it. He wanted his father to see him as a great man and he knew that if John Hartwell were alive today, he would be proud of him, provided he could win Garrett's U.S. Operations slot.

For over a year Harry had been putting together a proposal for a massive marketing and test program for ethanol in filling stations across the country, including a series of grassroots ethanol production refineries. As far as he could tell, ethanol—grain alcohol, in contrast to wood alcohol, called methanol—was the fuel of the future. As petroleum supplies in the bowels of the earth quickly ran out, and as environmentalists pressured automakers to find new, less polluting fuels for motor vehicles, ethanol or some variant of it would surface, even over methanol, as the preferred, renewable fuel. He wanted Ramoco to be the world leader in its production and distribution. In a word, Harry's proposal would mean an entirely new industry for Ramoco. "A New Fuel for a New Century" was the motto he planned to use.

He had done his homework carefully and built a cogent case for proceeding with the large-scale marketing and test program as well as with the grassroots ethanol production refineries. At today's meeting, he would be asking the board members for authorization to pursue this course of action. He hoped they would give him the authority both to develop the process technology and to design facilities for producing ethanol in half a dozen places across North America.

He knew his selling task would not be an easy one. Sitting on this board were some very tough-minded people. They demanded accuracy in details and thorough research. Many managers making new capital project proposals had left just such meetings red-faced and frustrated because they had not done their homework, and had been royally chewed out for it.

With a mixture of excitement and apprehension, Harry pulled into a space at the Ramoco headquarters parking lot, picked up his briefcase, and walked inside the building. The meeting was scheduled for ten o'clock, so he had at least an hour to make his final preparations. His ethanol project was the third item on the agenda.

Ann Laney was there already. She had found an office for him, a quiet place to go over his notes for the last time. With her preparing overhead transparencies and summary pages, he was sure there would be no errors in the materials to be shown or handed out.

He thanked her again for her unique research contribution to his project. In her father's attic, she had discovered a series of articles promoting "power alcohol," the farmers' name for fuels like methanol and ethanol, in a magazine called _Acres U.S.A._ In its pages she had found pieces of information that would give a special sparkle to his presentation, for example, that B-29 bombers in World War II flew on a fuel mixture including 100-proof power alcohol, that some racing cars in the Indianapolis 500 use 40 to 75 percent alcohol in their engines, and that the world's speedboat record was made with 100 percent alcohol fuel.

At ten minutes before ten, Harry gathered his papers together, walked out the door, and proceeded down the hall to the board room.

Some of the members had already arrived. He shook hands with Dr. Janet Mason, dean of the college of business at the local university, and then chatted for a moment with Jerry Hanford, the president of Citizens Bank. In addition to J. Lawrence Babcock, Jr. and three other senior vice presidents on the board, Harry said hello to Neil Curtis, Connie Marucca, and Joel Silverman.

A few seconds before ten, Carl Harris walked in. With pale blue eyes and brown hair combed in a ruler-straight part, he looked like the dour headmaster of a strict prep school. He closed the door behind him and went directly to his seat without shaking hands with anyone.

"As if he were in charge of the meeting!" thought Harry indignantly.

Harry had a hard time concentrating on the first two agenda items, so preoccupied was he with his own proposal.

The first item had to do with fifty-million-dollars of capital improvement for offshore drilling in the Gulf of Mexico. Harry knew about this and supported it. Carl was handling all the financial details. "He gets his fingers into every pie," thought Harry.

The next item had to do with union contracts, a big headache that came up periodically. The issue this time was whether to lock out union members if they failed to respond favorably to proposed hourly wage cutbacks. Ramoco had done a good job of cutting back as many salaried employees as possible and still maintaining high levels of productivity and standards of quality. According to the general sentiment of higher management, it was time for the unions to bite the bullet, and it remained to be seen what their level of willingness would be. Carl was the featured presenter, since he was the one who knew all the facts and figures.

"That guy is tied into everything that comes down the pike in Ramoco," thought Harry. "Even in my ethanol proposal, every cost estimate has come under his scrutiny."

It was nearly eleven o'clock when Harry was given the floor to make his presentation.

He felt extremely confident as he recited the steps he had taken leading up to this proposal. He had been negotiating for over a year with the management of Brady Ethanol Inc., a small but highly respected company on the cutting edge of fuel research. Brady had perfected the process technology for ethanol that Ramoco needed, and they were willing to sell Ramoco the exclusive rights to their chemical process, the secret formula that would create the new fuel industry. The heart of their secret was a new high-efficiency packing in the distillation column, which would allow them to feed in a mixture of 50% ethanol and 50% butyl alcohol and, at the end of the process, collect a 99.5% high-purity ethanol, ideal for automotive fuel. Moreover, Harry predicted that Brady's young staff of highly-qualified technicians, scientists, and engineers, who would be working with Ramoco engineers in the early design phase and start-up operations, would infuse new life into the Ramoco system.

"It looks like a sure winner and a natural marriage," was the way Harry summed up the history of the proposed project to the top brass sitting before him.

He proceeded through certain process-engineering details, pausing only briefly to answer a few questions from the floor. As he looked around the room, he could tell that the board members were impressed and interested, so his confidence grew.

Then he came to the most critical elements of his proposal: How much was this acquisition going to cost? How would the production teams be integrated? How would the transition from gasoline to ethanol be made at the pumps? What were the projections on future income from ethanol marketing in five, ten, and fifteen years? How long before the new facilities would pay for themselves and bring a return on investment for Ramoco?

In his preparation, Harry had been very careful to anticipate these questions and to provide as much detail as possible. He felt confident with his estimates and predictions, because Carl's staff had provided him with most of the financial details, costs estimates, economic evaluations, and the rest.

Then, in the middle of his presentation on the future earning potential of the ethanol project, Carl interrupted him.

"Those figures you're giving us, Harry, are incorrect."

There was a sudden silence in the room.

"Incorrect?" asked Harry. "That's nice to know," he added coldly.

"Those figures are not up-to-date," Carl replied. "It's as simple as that."

"Now, how could I have gotten out-of-date figures from your staff?" asked Harry.

"Those were early projections I gave you many months ago, and you never bothered to come back in the last few weeks to get updated projections based on more current market forecasts. I know you're aware that the cost of crude per barrel has taken a plunge of late."

"Expecting your office to send me updated figures was a bit to much to ask, I guess."

As the two men glared at each other, Harry recalled a time when Carl had called one of his ideas "half-baked," then patted him on the shoulder with a tinge of derision and annoyance as if Harry had been nothing more than a harmless, barking puppy. Carl never treated Harry as an equal.

He was standing in a pool of embarrassment. Carl had just intercepted his pass and was running, free and clear, toward his own goal for a sure touchdown.

Harry had to say something, because, if he didn't and let Carl's challenge be the last word, the board members would follow Carl's statement to its apparently logical conclusions, that the ethanol project was not a good business decision, and that Harry was not a good man to entrust with U.S. Operations. He saw his dilemma immediately. At worst, his proposal would be rejected; at best, he would be publicly embarrassed and told to go back and redo his calculations. In either case, it was good-bye to the big promotion.

"Remind me to leave my phone number with your secretary just in case you want to share some other important information with me," Harry frowned.

Carl stood up and told Harry to be quiet and listen for a minute.

"Here are some facts you didn't put into your proposal, Harry," he began. "First, according to recent studies, the worldwide oil glut will continue for the next two to three years with OPEC unable to prevent lower dollar-per-barrel costs. This means the American people won't need to look for a substitute for gasoline. Second, contrary to your suggestion, the American people are not environmentally motivated. They may claim they are, but studies show they don't act according to their claims. Third, for the next five years ethanol would continue to cost the consumer far more per gallon than gasoline and give far lower engine performance than gasoline. People at the pumps would realize they were being offered poorer performance for a higher price, and they wouldn't buy it. Harry, your vision that ethanol would be offered at every service station as an alternative to lead-free gasoline is a pipe dream. No matter how we tried to promote it, people wouldn't go for it."

Carl's eyes swept over the assembled board members faces as he gave his conclusion.

"The ethanol project which Harry is proposing would be a terrible strategic mistake for Ramoco. All ideas are not created equal, and this one is dumber than most. People do not want to put corn in their cars!"

With that, Carl sat down.

The rest of the staff looked uncomfortable—Neil Curtis, Connie Marucca, and Joel Silverman—none of them would dare look directly at Harry, yet they all glanced out of the corners of their eyes to see what was written on his face. On one level, they wished someone would call a halt to the battle; on another level, they wanted to see a fight to the finish, just to see how it would all turn out.

"An officer is pretty dumb when he doesn't recognize where the battle lines are drawn," said Harry quietly to Carl. "I should have covered my flanks."

Carl's lips curled into a victory grin, which only Harry could see.

Harry saw his future and his dreams going down the drain.

Sir Lawrence gave him a reprieve.

"We've put in a full morning," said the CEO. "We all need a change of pace. Let's continue discussing Harry's proposal after lunch. See you all at one o'clock."

—◆◈◆—

"**H**ow do you feel about the board meeting?" asked the Woman gently, as Harry walked down the corridor to the office that Ann Laney had set aside for him.

"I feel totally screwed by that scumbag Harris— that's how I feel!" whispered Harry, gritting his teeth. "In all the months I've been working on this project, he never even gave me a hint that he opposed it."

In the room, he continued, "I guess I shouldn't have turned my back. My biggest fault was in trusting him. I trusted Carl to give me the information that I needed. I trusted him to be a loyal colleague, and he turned out to be a conceited, malicious, underhanded traitor."

"But what happened at the board meeting, Harry?" the Woman asked again.

"I did what I was supposed to do," said Harry. "I had a well-thought-out plan for a project that would enhance the status, prestige, and profitability of Ramoco, and I was proud of what I had done. It didn't come out the way I wanted it to because of betrayal, pure and simple."

"So," the Woman asked, "you do not feel responsible for what happened at the board meeting this morning?"

"Absolutely not!" Harry retorted. "Why should I?"

"Why do you suppose Carl did what he did?" she asked. "Why do you suppose he wasn't loyal to you? Why would he betray you and seek to destroy you in the eyes of the other board members?"

"Because he's in it for himself, that's why!" he said.

"Carl is going to be involved with Ramoco for a long time. So, whether you like it or not, you two will be working together, maybe even side by side, in the same company for many years to come."

"What are you trying to say to me?"

"That Carl Harris is your final exam in managing from the heart."

"Wait just a minute!" shouted Harry. "That's not fair."

"Fair or not, he is your final exam today," the Woman said squarely. "And so far, your score on the five principles is not very high."

"I can't believe this!" cried Harry. "I'm already involved in the biggest test of my life in that boardroom, and you want to double the stakes? Not only my career, but now my life hangs in the balance! Have a heart, will you!"

"It's your turn to have the heart, Harry," replied the Woman. "I'm counting on you. It's time for you to show the board what your heart is made of. Remember, you've been practicing managing from the heart for six months, living out each of the principles at home and in the office. Why stop now?"

"Do you actually think I can go in there after lunch and manage Carl from the heart? That's asking a miracle."

"Not really, Harry," replied the Woman. She wanted Harry to succeed, but wasn't completely sure he could. And he certainly wouldn't, unless she did her coaching job very well, so she returned to her task. "Basically, it takes a little concentration and effort, as you have been telling your son—the way the two of you used to play one-on-one basketball in your back yard. You can win this final round, Harry, I know you can. You can manage Carl from your heart. Come on, acknowledge the greatness within yourself."

"Are you guaranteeing to support me when I get back in that boardroom?"

"What good am I as a teacher if my star pupil doesn't get an A?" she replied. "Of course, I'll be inside your head and your heart, marking your success every step of the way."

"I guess this is the supreme test," Harry said.

"You might call it that."

"If I can use these principles with Carl, I can use them with anyone." He banged the desk with his fist to announce this realization.

"It will be your biggest challenge yet, Harry. You'll really have to stretch, but you can do it. And, remember, if you succeed, it means your heart is whole and you're on your own."

"What's going on here?" asked Harry, realizing that the terrain of his mind was changing shape as he watched it. "Everything feels upside down. I must be going crazy. I'm supposed to be fighting for my career in that meeting, and here I am planning to open my heart to a guy who is ready to sink me into oblivion."

"That's right, Harry," the Woman exhorted. "You are going to hear Carl and understand him. You will tell him the truth with compassion. You will not make him wrong, even if you disagree. You will look for his loving intentions. And acknowledge the greatness within him. Relating to him from your heart will be your main objective when you go back into that meeting."

A kind of transformation began to come over Harry Hartwell in the following moments. Thoughts that seemed alien to him before became clear and felt at home in his mind. A brilliant light went on inside him, and Harry could see. What he saw was the rightness of managing from the heart.

"Yes!" he exclaimed. "That's right! Exactly right!"

Later, he would be hard-pressed to give an explanation of what had happened in his body and feelings in that moment of realization when he finally understood what the Woman had been teaching him all these months. The five principles were not just a coat of paint on life, they were the very foundation of it. Thoughts, feelings, and awarenesses kept tumbling all around inside Harry, and it was difficult for him to sort them out. He tried talking to himself to get his bearings.

"Sure, the ethanol project is important," he said to himself, "and I will fight for it, because I believe in it. But being a whole human being is much more important. And whether or not the ethanol project sinks or floats, I want to be true to myself. And I will relate to Carl from the heart, because I can be fully human only by relating to him from the heart."

"What kind of a relationship would you really like to have with Carl?" she asked, realizing that a major shift had taken place inside Harry. "Think of the best relationship with him you can imagine and go for it."

Harry's imagination created a picture of him and Carl working happily together side by side. Harry smiled at the image and shook his head in disbelief. "Is this what you have been trying to teach me all along?" he asked the Woman.

"Managing from the heart is not a series of techniques to get other people to do what you want them to do. It's a way of life. It's the only way to really live."

"I think I've finally got it," said Harry. "I'm ready for my final exam now."

———————————◆••◆—◆———————————

There was a bit of tension in the room after lunch, as Babcock called the meeting to order. He was not one to be put off by emotional stress in a group. Actually, he rather enjoyed a bit of jousting among the knights of his round table.

When the meeting resumed, most people expected that Harry would be dressed for war, have his armor on, and his lance aimed at Carl.

"Let me see if I grasped your main points, Carl," Harry began with a Listening Check. "Your opposition to the ethanol project is based on the fact that people won't buy ethanol currently because of its high cost and mediocre quality as a fuel, despite its environmental value."

"That's a pretty good summary of my position," acknowledged Carl warily, not sure where Harry was coming from or where he was going.

"I took a couple of shots at you before lunch, and I apologize for them," said Harry. "Now that I've reflected over what you said, I realize that, when all is said and done, you want the best for our company, you want to protect its interests, and you won't let me or anyone else steer it on a course that might do it serious harm."

All the eyes of the group were focused on a Harry they had never seen or heard before.

"I know," continued Harry, "that your intention this morning, as the responsible financial officer of this company, was to keep the company from making a bad financial mistake. When I look at it that way, I can appreciate why you said what you did about the ethanol project. You were concerned and were watching out for all of us, because all of us would have lost if any one of us made a major financial error."

"That's exactly right," said Carl, still unsettled by Harry's approach. "I'm glad you see it."

Carl was sure Harry had some trick up his sleeve. Nevertheless, he was hearing Harry restate his position accurately, clearly, and with understanding.

Now, Harry would tell him the truth with compassion.

"The truth is, Carl," Harry resumed, "what you're saying is right for the present time, this year, maybe even for the next five or so years. But I'm concerned about the future farther out than that. You know as well as I that, sooner or later, maybe twenty years down the road, oil will be in short supply. The Mideast wells will run dry. And the greenhouse effect will worsen. I believe we have to prepare ourselves for any of these eventualities, and that ethanol, or something very much like it, can play an important role in our future. If solar energy were ready, we probably might not have to go the ethanol route. But, so far, the potential of solar fuel to run automobiles is quite limited. So, I want us to get the jump on the competition with ethanol, to get experience producing it and marketing it. When we need it five or ten years from now, I want Ramoco to be ready, not caught with its pants down."

Carl reluctantly admitted that Harry had a point, but insisted that the arguments he had presented before lunch still held.

"Carl," said Harry, "even though the chemistry between us is pretty explosive sometimes, I acknowledge that you are a great financial wizard and that Ramoco wouldn't be in the enviable position it is now if it weren't for you. That's why I want you on the side of the ethanol project. You are so bright that, hardly trying, you were able to tear a lot of my work to shreds this morning. On the other hand, you are smart enough to know, deep down, that the project is something worthwhile for people and this planet. I want to enlist your financial greatness, not in demolishing the project, but in helping us design and build it in a manageable way. It would be easy for you to make it fail, but I think you are the one person who could help make it succeed."

Carl was silent.

Connie Marucca turned to Carl and asked, "What if we tried this ethanol project in just one region, say, the Midwest where corn grows and is considered a valuable part of life?"

"To try it in every state of the union at one time would be a recipe for disaster," said Carl, putting the project in perspective. "Most gas stations would give us a flat-out NO if we suggested they convert to ethanol, and the rest of them would go broke trying to sell the stuff."

"You're saying that to attempt selling the idea nationwide would be too massive a gamble?" replied Harry.

"Right," answered Carl, "and I'm not ready to gamble company money on such risky business."

"How about a few states, as Connie suggested?" asked Harry. "Could you take that much of a gamble?"

"Possibly," replied Carl.

"How about Iowa, Kansas, and Nebraska?" asked Connie.

"I would have to think about it."

"Carl," said Harry, "I want to thank you for considering the ethanol project and suggesting some ways we might implement it."

Carl gave a perfunctory nod.

Then, turning to Babcock, Harry said, "I request that my proposal be sent back for more research. If it's okay with Carl and the rest of the board, I would like you to assign Carl and me to work together to see if the project is something that Ramoco could and should do. Whatever is proposed, we can all be sure that Carl will never put the company at risk."

Then, turning to Carl, he said, "It seems you and I have mostly been at odds with each other up till now. I'd like to get to know you working together toward a shared goal."

There was a buzz in the group.

"What do you think of Harry's offer?" Babcock asked Carl.

"A total surprise," Carl replied honestly. "Off the wall."

"But, would you be willing to try it?" asked the CEO. "Working in partnership with Harry, I mean?"

Carl looked at Harry.

Harry smiled and waited.

"I'll give it a try," said Carl, shrugging his shoulders.

"Good," replied Babcock. "I admire both of you. Now, let's get to the next item on the agenda."

———◆◆◆———

"You did it, Harry," said the Woman proudly when he was back in his office at the refinery. "You managed Carl from the heart. All I had to do was enjoy watching you."

"I did it," replied Harry incredulously, raising his hand in victory. "I made statements in there that have never come out of my mouth before, and they all felt natural and right. The things I said to Carl today were totally unlike me, and yet they felt totally right and true."

"It took Carl a few minutes to get used to the new Harry," she said, chuckling, "but in the end he warmed up to you."

"Wouldn't it be ironic if he and I became good friends?" he mused, as he paced around the room, full of energy.

"It looks quite likely to me," commented the Woman.

He paused to look out the window.

"You know, I think I'm going to like working with him," he said. Then, turning back to face the center of the room, he added, "It's certainly better to have him on my side than against me."

"I predict that, as friends, both of you will be winners."

"I wonder what Babcock thought about that last scene between Carl and me?" he asked.

"I think he admired you very much," replied the Woman, "and he may seek you out for more important things. After all, there aren't many people in a company who can snatch victory from the jaws of defeat, and then convert the enemy leader to their side."

He sat down in an easy chair and grew silent.

The Woman remained quiet, too.

"I guess you have to go now," said Harry, bringing up the inevitable topic of separation. "I will really miss you."

"I will miss you, too," she replied. "However, you've earned your unconditional discretion, and I must move on to my next challenge."

"Challenge? Is that what you call guys like me?" asked Harry.

"I have admired your honesty every step of the way," she replied. "Unlike a lot of people in the world today, you are not a phony, Harry. You're a thoroughbred. Whether I had your cooperation or your resistance— and I've had them both—I always had them one hundred percent."

"You *do* realize that I'm totally changed?" he said. "I'm no longer the person you first met in that shiny white waiting room, wherever it was."

"I do realize it, Harry. The more important thing is that *you* realize it."

"From working with you, I've learned what heart is and how I'm connected to everyone," he said. "And, now that I've passed my test, I know that your going away isn't really a departure as much as it is starting a new way of relating to each other. Isn't that right?"

"It is a sort of commencement."

"How about for you?" he said, focusing his attention on her. "I'll bet I was some kind of final exam for you."

The Woman laughed. He was right.

"You know," he began, "I never told you before but—you know Neil Curtis, the V.P. for Human Resources—you remind me of him. Sometimes you sound a lot like him. Before now, I've never been able to understand him and where he was coming from. I think I know now. By the way, did you or one of your colleagues in the discretionary world ever put Neil through this managing from the heart training?"

"Funny you should ask."

"How many persons like you are around doing this training?"

"We have quite a team," she replied noncommittally. "Would you be interested in joining us?"

"No thank you," he replied without hesitation. "But I certainly will promote your work and use it in my life."

They both laughed.

"I'm beginning to really enjoy life," said Harry with a sigh that came from the bottom of his heart.

"To life, Harry! I toast your life."

"Good-bye, Selena. Thank you."

Epilogue

One month later, Harry was sitting intently at his desk scribbling on a yellow pad, when Ann Laney came in with the day's messages and correspondence.

"Good morning, Mr. Hartwell," she said. "Beautiful day out there."

Harry replied with a cheery, "Good morning, Ann," without looking up.

As she walked over to put the mail on his desk, her eyes focused on the yellow pad and a numbered list he had made on it.

"Some new ideas for the staff meeting today?" she asked. "Or for your Chamber of Commerce speech next week?"

Harry chuckled at her questions and pointed to what he had written.

"It's not for the Chamber of Commerce, nor is it for the meeting—at least not today's, Ann. Actually it's my new management credo."

He lifted the pad and she read the words aloud:

MANAGING FROM THE HEART

1. *Please don't make me wrong,*
   even if you disagree.
2. *Hear and understand me.*
3. *Tell me the truth with compassion.*
4. *Remember to look for my loving intentions.*
5. *Acknowledge the greatness within me.*

When she had finished reading the principles, she turned to look at Harry and waited.

"For a while now," he said as if sharing a secret, "I've tried acting as if each employee had made all five of those requests of me. I've come to think that my most important job as a manager is to meet those requests."

Ann's eyes widened. "So, that's what you've been up to," she exclaimed. "Everybody's been commenting on how much you've changed since your heart attack, but I never understood the pattern of your behavior before.

How did you arrive at these five principles? Where did they come from?"

Harry fidgeted a bit. "Well, in my case, I just had to figure out what the opposite was to an Abominable NO Man."

Ann gasped. "You know about that name?"

Harry laughed. "Yes," he conceded, "for years. And worse, I used to be proud of it. But now I think it will quickly become obsolete. I'm actually hoping the other people around here will pick up on these five principles and give them a try. If I can learn to use them, anyone can," he concluded, laughing at an image of his former abominable self.

"This surely would be an amazing place if all of us were able to use them," she acknowledged. "But aren't you worried about the effect on production?"

"You bet I was, at first," Harry agreed. "But now I'm convinced that the five principles support both productivity and morale. The trial period has been too short for any firm conclusions, but so far the evidence is encouraging."

Ann picked up the pad and read the words again. "'Managing From the Heart.' Pretty powerful stuff."

"Even though those five principles have changed my life," he said, "I have a dickens of a time trying to remember them. That's why I have the list on my desk. Otherwise, I keep forgetting one or another of them."

"I could type them for you, but I don't imagine that would help."

"Just now I've been trying to see if I can come up with a memory device by tying together the first letter of each principle, but PHTRA doesn't make any sense."

"My kids like to play a scrambled word game," said Ann as she leaned over the desk to look at the list again. "They try to make sense out of a jumble of letters. Would it make a difference if you changed the order of the principles?"

"Well, I learned them in this order, but I practice them in any order."

"Let's see," said Ann as she wrote different combinations—THRAP, TRAPH, PARTH, PHART, HARTP—on her note pad. "These last two show a part of your last name," she said, circling the letters, but that's not enough. In the game my children play, the letters usually spell out an ordinary word."

"It's close to HEART," he said. "Just one letter is wrong. If only 'Please Don't Make Me Wrong' started with an E."

"But it does," she said, smiling. "Simply switch the principle around to read: 'Even if you disagree, please don't make me wrong.'"

"That's it, Ann. I think it will work." He scribbled on his notepad.

MANAGING FROM THE HEART

H ear and understand me.

E ven if you disagree,
please don't make me wrong.

A cknowledge the greatness within me.

R emember to look for my loving
intentions.

T ell me the truth with compassion.

He held it up for her to look.

"It's great, Harry!"

"It was your idea."

"I play this game every day with my kids."

He closed his eyes and began reciting the principles. "I think I can remember all five of them now."

"Would you like me to have my friend print them in calligraphy and frame them for your wall?" she asked.

He nodded. "It would be a wonderful reminder of the six most important months in my life."

He glanced at his watch and rose from his desk.

"Time to go, Ann. I don't want to be late for our weekly senior staff meeting."

When Harry and Ann arrived at the Ramoco Board Room, Jim Weiss and all the department heads were already there. Harry noticed they were smiling at each other. They seemed happy to be together.

They smiled a welcome to Harry when they saw him come in.

Harry felt the group's openness to him, their understanding, their eagerness, their loving intentions. How different their spirit was from six months ago.

"Yes," Harry thought, "the evidence in favor of managing from the heart is very encouraging. I can really feel the greatness of the people here, and I know I can count on them."

Harry was very happy at how his life had turned out.

He greeted the group effusively.

"Good morning, folks! What a *beautiful* day!"

Managing From the ♥

H ear and understand me.

E ven if you disagree,
  please don't make me wrong.

A cknowledge the greatness
  within me.

R emember to look for my loving
  intentions.

T ell me the truth with compassion.

About the Authors
Hyler Bracey

Hyler Bracey's life journey has taken him from the cotton fields of Mississippi to President of The Atlanta Consulting Group. After doing everything from working on a tugboat and racing stock cars to owning a pair of cotton gins, in 1972 he formed the company along with Aubrey Sanford. Today the firm has grown from the two person operation to approximately forty people, with Fortune 500 clients all over the world. Having survived a serious racing accident, Hyler has become an inspirational leader and is helping The Atlanta Consulting Group move toward the following vision:

> _We are a loving, supportive team of top professionals._
> _We empower people to create organizations with_
> _vision, harmony, commitment and inspired results._
> _Integrity and dealing from the heart are our highest_
> _values._
> _Our work is fun and exciting and brings wealth,_
> _respect and joy in abundance to us and the people we_
> _touch._

Hyler received his Ph.D. from Louisiana State University in 1969 in management, marketing and finance. Prior to that he earned an MBA from the same institution in 1965 and a Bachelor of Business Administration/Marketing from Lamar University in 1964.

Hyler enjoys snow-skiing, snorkeling, white-water rafting, backpacking, and attending NASCAR races.

Jack Rosenblum

Jack Rosenblum is a nationally known management consultant who for over twenty years has been helping top teams learn to work together in harmony. He has a special gift for helping people embrace and work through conflict all the way to the end and come out the other side as allies and friends. He does this with married couples as well as with work teams.

Jack received an Ed.D. in organization development from the University of Massachusetts in 1977. He earned a J.D. from Yale Law School in 1962 and an A.B. from Brown University in 1959.

He joined The Atlanta Consulting Group as Vice President, Research and Development in 1983. In prior careers, he was President of RSI, Inc., a management consulting firm; Chief of New York City's drug prevention program for youth; and one of the first Peace Corps volunteers in Costa Rica.

He is a dedicated tennis buff, bicyclist and skier, a voracious reader of fiction and non-fiction, and an avid movie-goer.

Aubrey Sanford

Aubrey Sanford came from a small southern town and, through dedication and more than a little innate talent, has become one of the most entertaining, beloved and effective seminar leaders in the country. Joining with Hyler to create The Atlanta Consulting Group in 1972, Aubrey developed the knack of taking concepts like motivation, coaching and listening, and devising ways for people to learn those skills experientially. His design work is reflected in all TACG workshops.

Aubrey received a Ph.D. in Business Administration from Louisiana State University in 1970 after earning an MBA from the University of Southern Mississippi in 1966. He has co-authored three previous books: _Human Relations: Theory and Practice_; _Organizational Communication and Behavior_; and _Basic Management and the Experiential Approach_.

His hobbies include skiing and working on classic Mustang cars.

Roy Trueblood

Roy Trueblood brings over three decades of counseling experience to The Atlanta Consulting Group. An ordained United Methodist minister, psychotherapist and professor of counseling in previous careers, Roy has a special gift for helping people enhance their self-esteem and learn how to enhance the self-esteem of others. He has contributed a lot of the heart to The Atlanta Consulting Group and its workshops.

Roy received a Ph.D. in counseling and psychology from Northwestern University in 1972 and a B.D. in religion from the Garrett Theological Seminary in 1961. He joined The Atlanta Consulting Group as Vice President in 1977.

Roy has a passion for Thoroughbred race horses and can also be found on a bicycle or skis.

Services Available

Hyler Bracey, Jack Rosenblum, Aubrey Sanford, Roy Trueblood and The Atlanta Consulting Group work together to help people create organizations with vision, harmony, commitment and inspired results. This book is only one of their services. Their expertise is concentrated in five areas:

❏ Organization and culture change projects (at corporate and operating unit levels).

❏ Senior and upper level executive development (with emphasis on intact management teams).

❏ Internal <u>and</u> external customer/supplier interaction (as a component of Total Quality management).

❏ Management and supervisory leadership training (tied to strategic organization initiatives).

❏ "Breakthrough Living" Program (used to achieve positive life balance and to demonstrate an organization's concern for its people).

If you would like further information about any of these services you may contact:

The Atlanta Consulting Group
2028 Powers Ferry Road
Suite 190
Atlanta, Georgia 30339
404/952-8000